Ruth Baetz met her first lover in college and lived with her for five years in a very closeted relationship.

When that love affair ended, Ruth turned to her community for love and support. As she worked to learn about living openly as a Lesbian, she began to realize that these steps to community, life and wholeness must be taken by every Lesbian no matter what circumstances compel her "coming out."

Ruth interviewed over eighty women and finally chose fifteen from widely varying backgrounds to make up the women of LESBIAN CROSSROADS.

These women share their personal lives in intimate detail in the pages of LESBIAN CROSSROADS, becoming, in fact, a part of the community of every Lesbian's life.

An exciting, richly rewarding experience! A roadmap leading to your own people.

ABOUT THE AUTHOR

Ruth Baetz and her lover live in the Pacific Northwest where they are avid nature lovers, feminist activists and homebodies. Ruth has a private therapy practice in Seattle where she specializes in women's issues and counseling lesbians. She also gives workshops on counseling lesbians, coming out to parents, meeting your inner child, etc.

Lesbian Crossroads

By Ruth Baetz

NAIAD PRESS
1988

Library of Congress Cataloging-in-Publication Data

Baetz, Ruth.
  Lesbian crossroads.

  Reprint. Originally published: New York:
Morrow, 1980.
  1. Lesbians—United States—Biography.   I. Title.
[HQ75.3.B34   1988]   306.7′663′0922   88-18032
ISBN 0-941483-21-5

To the Lesbian Movement

Preface

Imagine that your sister's friend is writing a book about heterosexuals and you have agreed to be interviewed. She is very serious in asking you these questions and needs well-thought-out answers.

There are only three major questions:

1. What is your definition of a heterosexual? (Is it a political stand? A lifestyle? Sexual attraction whether acted upon or not?)

2. How did you come to realize you are a heterosexual?

3. What did you have to deal with after you realized it?

Some things to consider in answering these questions might be: What had you heard about heterosexuals before you realized you were one? Had you ever met one?

How long did it take for you to accept that label? How long did you try to be homosexual, bisexual, celibate?

Have you told your parents you are heterosexual? If not, how do you keep it from them? If so, how did you do it?

How has telling or not telling affected your relationship with them?

Have you told your sisters and brothers? Other relatives?

How have you dealt with telling or not telling your children?

Did you have any religious conflicts when you realized you were a heterosexual? If so, how have you resolved them?

How have therapists reacted to your heterosexuality? Have they tried to cure you? Have they taken you seriously?

Did you let your schoolmates or teachers know you were heterosexual? How did they react?

Do your co-workers know? If so, how have they reacted? If not, how do you keep it from them? Have you told your boss?

Have you experienced discrimination or harassment for being heterosexual, and if so, how have you handled it?

Has realizing you're heterosexual changed your political views?

Did you have any cultural conflicts when you realized you were a heterosexual? Are people of your culture supportive of heterosexuality? Have you felt torn between working for the rights of your ethnic group and working for heterosexual rights?

How did you find other heterosexuals to relate to?

Would you ever have "come out" as a heterosexual if you had known you would have to deal with all these issues, make all these decisions, and take all these risks? Would you still be trying to be someone you're not in order to avoid this pain?

Acknowledgments

As one member of a worldwide Women's Movement and a Worldwide Lesbian/Gay Movement, I am very conscious that I as a lesbian could never have put my name on a book like this, let alone written it, without the work and support of the women before me and around me. We have created a climate of attitudes which have made possible both my personal process and the publication of this book.

Even within this climate, however, I could never have persevered without personal support. The consistent encouragement and editing skills of my good friend Nancy Manahan certainly qualify her as co-parent of the book. Nancy kept the spirit of the book alive through many of my discouraged times. The deadlines and feedback of the Napa Women's Writing group, and the support, patience, and enthusiasm of my friends Karen Vertin, Jan, and Maria Di Angelo were invaluable. Carol Murray's encouragement at a critical time truly meant the difference between giving up

9

and finishing the book. Deborah Hillwomon donated valuable personal, political, and artistic energy.

I would like to thank all the lesbians I interviewed for their time and positive energy. While I wasn't able to use even half of the interviews, your hospitality and personal stories were vital in forming the life of the book and inspiring my own sense of pride in our community. I appreciate the trust and caring it took to share your lives with unknown women across the country.

In addition, I'd like to thank the Pacific Center for Sexual Minorities in Berkeley, Gay Youth, the Lesbian Alliance of Santa Rosa, and Napa's Lesbian Support Group for valuable information and support.

Contents

Dealing with the World Around Us

Within Our Families

Introduction

This book has been part of a search for my own identity and my own community. The idea for it came at a crisis point in my life, a painful space between endings and new beginnings. My marriage was over, and I had no idea what lay ahead.

I had met my love in college, and we had lived together for five years. We considered ourselves married, although of course it was unofficial: we were both women. Never did I attach the label "lesbian" to either of us. I rarely thought of the term, and when I did I simply assumed that lesbians were women "out there" who were probably sick or deranged and at any rate were trying to be men. For myself, I was glad both Maria and I were women. Although I realized I would have to give up certain social and psychological freedoms for our relationship, it was a price I was willing to pay for personal happiness.

We had a classic "closet" marriage; we were an island

unto ourselves. We confided our love to only a few close friends and drew all our deep emotional support from each other. When we met our first lesbian friends two years after our marriage, I was relieved to find other women who loved each other, but I was also puzzled. These two women said they were lesbians, and yet they were as normal as we were.

Our social relationships didn't change much for the remaining three years of our marriage. Most of our friends, who were heterosexual, thought Maria and I were just good friends. The few lesbian friends we discovered in those years were as much in the closet as we were, and it was easy to rationalize that they were "special" (not really lesbians), just as we were "special."

Then Maria divorced me, and my island world collapsed. The next months can only be described as excruciatingly painful and confusing. When finally I began to think about a new life, a problem of unsuspected magnitude hit me: Where would I find the emotional support I needed? Time and again the answer came up, "From women," and I was terrified. Did that mean I was a lesbian? What would happen if I said out loud to someone, "I am a lesbian"? How would I find others like myself if I didn't say it out loud?

Searching for my sexual identity and trying to find out what it meant to be a lesbian in this society were the loneliest times I've ever known. As I stumbled through the scary stages of checking books about lesbians out of the library, stammering to a few trusted people that I was a lesbian, and beginning my search for other lesbians, I thought to myself over and over again, "No one should have to go through this alone. No one should have to face all the questions and fears without some kind of support group to share with and get answers from."

I decided to write this book. If I couldn't supply a support group for every woman to talk to about her sexual identity, then I could at least bring her a group of lesbians in a book who could share their experiences with her. Besides, I still had a lot of questions myself. What kinds of compromises did lesbians make so their lives could be as fulfilling as possible? What discrimination was out there, and how had other women avoided or dealt with it?

I began tentative interviews at this point, formulating questions and talking with the few lesbians I knew. The urgency to write the book waned, however, as I became more comfortable with my identity and had some gay friends. Then my mother learned I was a lesbian, and after we had exchanged wrenching letters for several months, she declared that I was retroactively aborted.

Months of pain followed, and this time I had some lesbian friends to support me. But again I felt cheated. Why hadn't I read that I might be disowned? How had other lesbians dealt with their parents? What had been my options in dealing with mine? And what else was out there in my future as a lesbian?

Next time, I wanted to know in advance what I might run into. I wanted information, not to copy someone else's actions, but to know the possibilities and how it did or didn't work out for people in circumstances similar to mine. I began to work on the book in earnest. No one should have to go through this alone.

As I began the interviews, I realized I was assuming that other lesbians' stories would be similar to mine. I assumed the women had come to a sudden realization and that it had changed their lives drastically as it had mine. However, I found that for some women the whole process was very gradual, while for others it happened in stages. I assumed that after realizing she was a lesbian, a woman would have to face all sorts of decisions as I had, and instead I found that some women weighed the decisions before accepting the identity. I assumed coming out was painful, while for some women it was joyful and easy.

After the first few interviews, I realized I had to drop my predetermined, limiting questions and ask a few general ones, letting the women themselves tell me what had been important to them. The two basic questions I asked were, "How did you come to realize you are a lesbian?" and, "What were the most important things you had to deal with after you realized it?"

I tried to avoid the term "coming out" because it means different things to different people. The women in the book who talk about coming out may be referring to their first sexual experience with a woman, to accepting the label of lesbian, to telling friends, or to announcing their lesbianism publicly. In all cases, "coming out" refers to a crossroad in their lives, a major change in consciousness, relationship, or lifestyle.

I especially want this book to reach those of you who are questioning your sexual identity. You are not alone. Many of us have asked ourselves the same questions, done the same searching as you are doing now. I want to give you some idea of how we came to identify ourselves as lesbians, what you may face as a lesbian, and how some of us have handled problems that arise.

However, this book is not only for women wondering whether or not they are lesbians. Every woman who comes into contact with the Women's Movement faces the question, "Who are these lesbians?" We are active workers in the movement, and with the International Women's Year Conference making a strong statement in support of gay rights, many heterosexual women have to face old prejudices and lack of knowledge about us.

As the issue of gay rights is debated and more and more lesbians publicly state their identities; families, friends, teachers, employers, ministers, counselors, politicians, and voters are all finding they need to know more about lesbian women. What do you say when someone tells you she's a lesbian? What has she gone through to get to the point of telling you? Here is an inside look into our lives, our fears, our choices, our joys. Understanding us may be more important to your life than you know right now because many of us—perhaps a woman close to you—are in the process of telling the people around us we are lesbians.

The interviews can also be helpful to lesbians who already accept their identity. On a personal level, they can suggest new ways to deal with such things as work situations, family relations, and religious conflicts. The process of "coming out" is a continual one, and although we may already have made it safely through some of these passages, moving to a new town or job will raise these issues again and require new strategies.

From a broader perspective, the interviews comprise chapters of our lesbian herstory: the lives and processes of other lesbians. Whether the women on these pages dealt with their identities twenty years ago or yesterday, their stories are not just personal accounts, but also a reflection of their times, locations, and the gay consciousness of the community around them. As we work together on an increasingly larger scale—citywide, statewide, nationwide—it's important to understand the range of our unique personalities and experiences.

Finally, this book is for students. Lesbianism is considered illegal and immoral in most sectors of society. The way lesbians deal with this status can be instructive to any student of psychology, sociology, or social work. How do we resolve the contradiction between what society says we are and what we know ourselves to be? How did we deal with being invisible? How do we find and adjust to a hidden subculture? We all formed our self-images and world views unconsciously in childhood. How do we lesbians now go about redefining ourselves and consciously constructing a new self-image and world view?

Many things are not covered by this book. I make no attempt to prove lesbianism is healthy or natural. That has been adequately explained by books currently on the market, and I take it as a given. This book goes one step further and looks into lesbians' lives, examining the extremely complex situations with which we must deal simply because our sexual preference falls outside the societal norm.

I want to caution the reader that this is only an overview of an enormous subject, and the wide range of lesbian experiences can only be partially represented in a book of this length. In order to explore a really thorough cross-section of experiences, I would need to interview women of every age, in every cultural minority, in every class, in every state, in every religion, in both city and country, who have realized their sexual identities at different times. Imagine the quantity. Now, there's no doubt the experience of a Black lesbian in the country is different from that of a white lesbian in the country, or that a Chicana lesbian's experience in Los Angeles is different from a Chicana lesbian's experience in Chicago. The woman who realized she was a lesbian a year ago at age sixty had a very different experience from the sixty-year-old who realized it twenty years ago, or from the woman who realized it a year ago at age twenty. Here you will get only a sampling of our diversity.

The women here are not representative of all lesbians in another important way. These women are survivors. They have not been physically coerced, or psychologically or religiously guilt-tripped out of their sexual preference. They have not been permanently institutionalized or killed. Nor have they committed suicide in despair. They have been strong, and they have been lucky.

In order to be part of this book, the women I interviewed had to be willing to take the label of lesbian. According to some women, under certain circumstances they would consider a woman a lesbian even if she didn't accept that label herself. For the purposes of this book, I do not. I had several long discussions with women who are opposed to labeling themselves in any way or who are opposed to calling themselves lesbians though sexually they relate exclusively to women. This book is not about them. This book is about women who call themselves lesbians, whatever that label means to them.

It is important to keep in mind that who I am as the interviewer and editor has biased the interviews. I am white, middle-class, twenty-eight, healthy, and college-educated. All these things affect how I relate to women I interview, whom I can find, whether my questions and reactions during the interview adequately evoke the important issues in the women's lives, how well I understand their perspectives, and what I think is important to include in the book. My background also affects how women relate to me, their willingness or unwillingness to be interviewed, and their openness during the interview. Although my aim is for each woman to tell her own story, I was there and I did the editing. She might have told her story slightly differently to you, and you might have found some points important which I did not include.

I would also like to stress that some of these women would tell their stories differently today, and I might ask other questions or edit them differently. We are all in process. The way we interpret our pasts changes as we change. Our attitudes about being a lesbian, or our definition of a lesbian, can change with time also. Here you have one frame in the films of several women's lives. In these frames you may catch us contradicting ourselves, coming to a new realization, denying something that seems quite obvious to you, reevaluating a theory—in short, doing all the things that people in process do.

Many people ask me how I went about finding lesbians to interview. I did it any way I could think of. I asked the lesbians I knew, and I asked them to ask their friends. I put ads in women's papers and asked for references from women's centers, women's bookstores, and gay groups. I responded to ads placed in papers by lesbians and asked if they knew of anyone I could interview. I traveled as far and as often as I could to do interviews, but my finances were limited so I had to rely on women who lived on or who were visiting the West Coast.

Generally, the interviews were taped in my home or in the women's homes, and most of the women had never seen me before. Some women wanted to be anonymous in the book and so have pseudonyms and altered biographical data. It was very important to me that the women felt free to expand on subjects that were most important to them and to avoid any they didn't want to discuss. The chapters here represent the areas women mentioned most often and which they said were most important to them.

Every interview that follows is a gift of time, emotional energy, and trust. With gay rights under attack throughout the country, it took a good deal of trust and courage to share with a stranger intimate feelings that would be published and distributed nationwide. The lesbians you will meet here, and many others I wasn't able to include, have taken that risk in order to reach out to you, hoping you can learn from their experiences and make the decisions you face at your lesbian crossroads easier for yourselves and your loved ones.

Within Ourselves

Realizations

You are about to meet fifteen lesbians who have agreed to share parts of their lives with you. In this section, they will talk about the process leading up to their realization that they are lesbians.

Each woman tells her own story and creates her own framework and definitions for her story. No one person has the answer to what a lesbian is or how to handle particular situations. My hope is that within the variety here you can find women to identify with or experiences that will clarify questions in your own lives.

I asked each woman to define the term lesbian, first of all so you can see how diverse our definitions of ourselves within that label are, and secondly so you have a framework for understanding each woman's life.

You will meet these women again in later chapters. If you find one you particularly identify with and you want to maintain the continuity of her life and circumstances, feel free to skip to her narration in the other chapters.

Carol Queen

WHAT IS YOUR DEFINITION OF A LESBIAN?

I would define a lesbian as a woman who relates in emotionally intimate and probably therefore physically intimate ways to other women. I think a woman can relate to men in sexual ways, and in friendship ways, but never really hit the peaks that she can with other women. I see lesbians as hav ing some kind of political consciousness. If you had asked me a hundred years ago, I would have come up with something completely different; but now, considering the dynamics of men to women, and men to men, and women to women, that's how I see it.

HOW DID YOU REALIZE YOU ARE A LESBIAN?

I began as an awkward, outside individual in a small town, and I was political when I was pretty young. When I was eleven I was writing "Lyndon Johnson is a ratfink" on my schoolbooks; so that shows what kind of consciousness I had. I lived vicariously because I felt that I was squelched in a small, conservative town, and I was restricted, except in my thoughts. My family was liberal enough and they really didn't restrict my reading, so I would journey to Woodstock in my head, and take part in Kent State in my head, because that was just my particular kind of fantasy life.

When I was in the eighth grade, the Women's Movement was getting into swing, and I became involved with that in an academic way, reading magazines and books, and proselytizing in high school and junior high. Then, when I was fourteen, the big hassle about lesbians within the Women's Movement, within N.O.W., hit the women's magazines. Just because I felt so involved with the Women's Movement to begin with, and because I felt so involved with oppression in everything, I figured I had to consider the lesbian issue seriously.

I hadn't really thought much about it before that, even though my classmates used to call me queer when I was in sixth grade because of my last name. They thought that Queen and queer were cute, and I encouraged them until my best friend Kristin told me what it meant. I thought it meant unusual, unique, possibly a notch above the others, an individual. She said, "No, that means homosexual." I said, "You're lying. I never heard that before, you must be lying." She said, "No, my mother told me." I said, "Where did your mother find out? Show me a dictionary with that in it." I was adamant that that couldn't be what it meant, but I discouraged them calling me queer from then on, because I figured they wouldn't see it quite the way I did. At that age, I didn't know if I was a homosexual or not, and I didn't give a damn, because I was involved in other head trips.

Later, when I started reading psychology, I found out that girls in early adolescence are supposed to experience crushes on classmates and teachers. I thought to myself, "Well, I know I've experienced crushes on boys, sort of a pain in the ass, but I know I have. But I've never felt anything like that for one of my girlfriends or one of my female teachers, so therefore I must be abnormal." I worried about that for a month, and then it passed.

So by the time I read the magazine articles about N.O.W., I was really emotionally detached from the idea of lesbianism. I just thought about it and said to myself, "Well, I know I'm attracted to men, could I be attracted to women, too?" I decided that probably I could, probably sometime that would happen, and I forgot about it.

My junior year of high school I went to a girls' school in

Germany. Since I was an outsider and didn't belong to any cliques or develop any close friendships in the school, I was able to sit back through five or six hours a day of classes that I wasn't really paying attention to and observe the other women in the school. I was observing, again, almost in an academic way, and I found myself becoming attracted to a few of them and to a couple of the teachers. I said to myself, "Oh, here is my adolescent homosexual phase coming finally."

At the same time, I was mad about this German guy who wanted to marry me and wanted to restrict me and wanted me to have children. It was the kind of relationship that I, as a budding feminist, had said that I would never become involved in. We went so far as almost becoming engaged, and yet I knew all the while that at any moment I could call my parents and say, "I think I'd better come home."

So here was this disgustingly romantic relationship with a guy on one hand, and then there was the almost pure level on which I was attracted to these women. I didn't feel able even to begin to initiate any kind of relationship with any of the women. In terms of language, what would I have been able to say? "I love you" was fine, but that didn't have any nuance to it whatever.

So I was safe, admiring and desiring and wanting to become closer to them but knowing that I really couldn't. When I came back home to my small-town high school, culture shock set in, and for a long time, again, I really didn't think about my attraction to the women.

At the end of the year, I went to Cannon Beach to be an apprentice in a summer-stock theater company. Another apprentice, my roommate, had just graduated from high school in a small town along the coast, and we had everything in common. We were even both wearing E.R.A. bracelets, which nobody in the state of Oregon had ever glimpsed

before. I fell madly in love. Barbara, however, was in love
with a man who was bound to fuck her up no matter which
way she turned. She would come home to me and cry on my
shoulder and say, "Oh, Carol, if only you were a man." I
wrote poetry and walked on the beach a lot.

We really did have a lot in common and became very close,
but there was always a continual element of frustration because she was very flirtatious. She knew damn well that I
was madly in love with her, and she loved it. A couple of
times we managed to talk about it rationally, and she re-
peated her statement: "I really wish you were a man. I
would be much more ready to relate to you on some kind
of deep level." She also said, "You know, I'm just in a different place. If you want to wait for me, fine." There it was.
I came to Eugene to go to the university—she went to school
at Antioch, Ohio—and I waited.

At Christmas, she came to spend time with me at my
parents' house, and we got very little sleep for two days.
It was the epitome of glory, right? Well, we didn't see each
other again until the next summer, and unfortunately Barbara was still very much attracted to men who weren't going
to appreciate her a bit. It seemed to me in my position of
jealous lover, which was how I saw myself, that she was just
asking to get screwed over at every step of the way.

During this time, I wanted to consider myself a lesbian,
but I knew if one were going to define me as anything,
that experientially I was, at best, a sort of low-grade bisexual.
I wanted to be called a lesbian because I had been glomming
down lesbian literature and gay literature of all kinds. I was
politically attracted to lesbianism, and yet I'd been reading
all the separatist literature that said, "Bisexual, huh-uh,
wrong. You're either deluded, or you're trying to escape from
something." I said, "No, no. Maybe I'm deluded, but I'm
not trying to escape from anything." So I became probably

the only hard-core political bisexual that the world has ever seen. This was the spring term of my freshman year at college.

I went through the familiar story of hanging around outside the Gay People's Alliance office on campus eight days a week, knowing just exactly who worked there, when they came and when they went, when the office was empty and when it wasn't, but not being able to step inside the door. Somehow I had developed this fear of rejection by political lesbians into such raging and mammoth proportions that I just knew if I walked in, they would take one look at me and say, "We can tell by looking at you that you haven't thrown out your diaphragm yet. Get out of here."

At the same time, I had all these rosy lavender fantasies. For example, the guy was supposed to grab my hand and say, "Come in. Here we are. We've been waiting for you. We are your community." Instead, when I finally womped up the courage to walk inside the office, he said, "Hi. What can I do for you?"

I said, "Um, can you tell me if, uh, uh, uh, is there a lesbian rap group at the Women's Center?" He said, "I think so, let me check my file box." So he checked his file box, and it took him an hour and a half; it must have. I was sitting there, shivering in my boots. (I was wearing boots, of course. Might as well look the part.)

Finally he said, "Yeah, I think there is." He gave me the phone number; then he called over the wall to another office and said, "Hey, what's-your-name, do you know when the lesbian rap group meets?" I thought, "Don't yell." But then I decided, "Well, I'm going to come out now, so he can yell if he wants to; everybody around here seems to be friendly enough."

I must have wasted six dimes before I finally let the call go through on the pay phone in my dorm. It was really odd. I was caught between the horns of a dilemma. I had a lot of men I cared about and liked to sleep with, and yet, "Women! God!" I didn't know if I could classify myself as gay. I felt gay, but what did that mean? I couldn't conceive of any middle ground right then.

I finally put the call through to the Women's Center and went to the lesbian rap group. I admired the women I saw there, but I felt like there was a sheet of glass a foot thick between me and them. They talked a lot about a panel they had been on that day, and I was eating it up, but I had no idea what I should say to make some kind of outreach. "Hi, I want you to validate me?" There was really nothing I could say that would sound halfway right.

My body language was amazing. I had not assumed such a fetal position since I left my mother's womb. Maybe they didn't know what to say to me. I have since discovered that in dealing with a young person who is scrunched up like that, it's hard to know where to begin. So they smiled at me and were friendly and said, "Oh, you look too young to go down to the bar with us." I said, "I'm seventeen." They said, "Aw, that's too bad. Well, when you're twenty-one, come on down to the bar."

They went to the bar, and I went home and experienced fits of frenzy all night. I was so frustrated. There they were. They were gorgeous, they were beautiful, I loved them, and I would see them in the bar when I was twenty-one. But in the meantime, I had four years to agonize. So I wrote letters to all my friends and ripped them up and said, "Oh, no, I can't send these; they won't know what I'm talking about."

Gay Pride week came, and I went to every panel and every activity and memorized everybody's face. From then on, whenever a gay person crossed campus I knew it. I said, "Aha! I know that person's gay. I sure feel warm and supportive toward that person, but, well, back up to my dormitory room to write more letters."

In the spring, the university offered its first term of a gay studies course. I was down at that registration table an hour before it even opened, and I was the first person to sign up for the class.

The first day everything fell into place. The teacher talked about definitions of gayness and about identity. She said, "There are as many different definitions for gay as there are people to define it, and if you consider yourself gay, then you are." Then she said, "And the same goes for lesbianism. I consider myself lesbian partially because it's a political and social statement and partially because it best describes the way I feel. I could sleep with eight men and only one woman and I would still call myself a lesbian, because that's the kind of statement it is."

Thunder crashed and lightning flashed, and it was a cosmic experience. Just that much validation, and wham, there I was, gay.

After that I went around campus saying, "I'm gay, I'm gay, I'm gay." I told a lot of people in the first two days. The straight people I ran into at that time were so supportive. If they had been nasty, I don't know how I would have reacted.

People said to me, "You seem to be getting a lot out of that class." And I'd say, "Oh, I am." I just blossomed. I sat there grinning throughout the class, sucking in all the information that I wanted so badly to receive. I was a gigantic human vacuum cleaner. I loved it.

I was born in 1957 in the fair city of Eugene, Oregon, and my family immediately moved to a remote farm in Cheshire, which is near Eugene. When I was ten, we moved to the rural town of Glide. This move was the great upheaval of my life and turned me into a political activist. I don't actually know how that happened, but it did. I went to high school there, spent my junior year in Germany, and attended the University of Oregon from 1974 to 1975, when I ran out of money.

I want to go back to school and major in sexuality counseling. I haven't exactly been doing counseling work, but I've been working with Gay Youth since I helped found it almost a year ago. I just turned nineteen.

Laverne Jefferson

WHAT IS YOUR DEFINITION OF A LESBIAN?

A lesbian is a lady who goes with a lady, or a lady that is attracted to a lady.

HOW DID YOU REALIZE YOU ARE A LESBIAN?

I guess I've known since I was six years old. My mom and dad had split up, you see, and my sister used to make me go to bed with her. From then on, I would always be attracted to ladies. I didn't know why, but every time I'd look at a lady I'd think, "Wow, she's cute."

When I was in eighth grade, I was attracted to all these ladies and wondered, "Why am I attracted to them so much?" I had this teacher that was like a mom to me, and she'd try to tell me what was happening. She would tell me all about the gay people, and I would think, "Well, maybe I'm gay because my mom left when I was six." I decided that that could have been part of it, but the feelings I had was too strong not to be.

I remember one time I was in juvenile hall. I was about fourteen, and I was in there for years, it seemed like. They can't keep you over six months at a time, but they did me. That was my home. I was in there for so long I started thinking, "Wow, I'm gonna do something." We had these little vents on our doors. What I and this other gay lady did

is we took the vents off so that we could crawl in and out.
So I had a relationship with that woman in and out of the
vents, but when I came out of juvenile hall, I'd sometimes
still see the little boys.

All this time, I was trying to figure out what I wanted.
I knew I was gay, but I was doing bisexual things. Before
I came out of the bisexual trip, I had a baby boy. It was just
like a Virgin Mary baby. I went to bed with the man and
stuff, but I didn't get anything out of it. I didn't feel anything. I was getting more from the women than I did from
the men, and I thought, "Aha!" So I just decided to change
my menu.

Right after I had my boy, I had a relationship with a
woman that lasted six years. I just decided that it was time
for me to do it, and I did.

I did three years in jail, and some of the women played
little games of being gay on the inside and straight on the
outside. But my lover got out before I did, and she waited
for me, and we just settled down.

It wasn't like I ever labeled it, it was just that I preferred
women. In those days, for Black people, you didn't put a
label on it. If you label it, then you gotta think, "What is my
dad gonna say?" People don't understand that there's a lot
of Black people running around here whose parents still
don't know, and they can be something like thirty, forty
years old, because it's just a different culture.

I don't really think it should have a label. Some people
say, "Are you a lesbian?" And I say, "No, I'm Laverne."
Because that's just like saying, "Are you a queer?" I'm not
queer, I just like women. They should call men that like
women queer; they're the queer ones.

I'm twenty-three. I grew up in a small town in Arizona.
My father was self-employed as a car dismantler. He'd junk

cars, smash them, and take them to the city to sell. My mom, what did she do? Nothing. Not a damn thing. She had us and she was gone and that was it. I went in and out of jails, taught a little school, and I'm trying to raise my son, and that's enough.

Jeri

WHAT IS YOUR DEFINITION OF A LESBIAN?

It's a woman-identified woman. It's hard to put in words because it's so all-encompassing. My whole life revolves around my relationship with a woman. It's an emotional, spiritual, sexual, intellectual relationship.

HOW DID YOU REALIZE YOU ARE A LESBIAN?

I'm not going to say I knew I was a lesbian when I was two years old, because I didn't. Like a lot of women, I knew I had feelings for other women but didn't know quite how to put a word on it. When I was ten, I probably had heavier crushes on friends than other girls in my class did. I would carry books home from school for a girlfriend and buy her candy bars.

When I was twelve, I went to church summer camp and had a mad, all-consuming crush on this other girl. When I told her I really liked her a lot, she said, "Well, that sounds kind of queer to me." I said, "What do you mean?" She said, "That's women that like other women. That's wrong." That was probably my first explanation of what I was feeling.

I felt a little uncomfortable, but it didn't change the way I felt about her at all. I continued seeing her after summer camp. We'd go to Youth for Christ together and kind of hug and neck in the back of the car when my parents were driving us home, which I can't understand. They didn't see, or what?

When I was in high school, it was acceptable for girls to touch and travel in packs, and there wasn't any pressure put on me to date. So I suppose it didn't really hit me until I was in my senior year of high school, and then I started questioning why I didn't get excited talking about boys the way my girlfriends did.

I came from a very religious family, so I had that to contend with: that it was a sin, besides not being socially acceptable. I would read through the Bible trying to find references to homosexuality, and it only reinforced the things I heard in church. My church didn't really talk about it that much, because it was so taboo they wouldn't even tell you it was wrong. At that point, I still thought it was something I could probably overcome.

I went steady with a guy in high school and continued seeing him the year after I got out of high school. He joined the service, and after a year of exchanging letters I went to see him in Germany. We thought we were going to get married, but when I could not sexually bring myself to go to bed with him, I finally had to say, "I don't love you. Whatever it was I thought I felt was just something I thought I was supposed to feel."

On that trip, I met a woman in Germany who had been my pen pal since I was nine years old. We went on a vacation to Spain together, and one thing led to another and she asked me what I thought about women loving women. We hadn't ever talked about it before. I said, "Why?" She said, "Well, because I think I love you."

We ended up having a relationship, but it was not sexual because she could not bring herself to any kind of genital contact All the feelings I had penned up inside me since I was ten finally culminated in that kind of response from her. It was very frustrating for both of us. She came from a very religious family, similar to my background.

At that time, I was going through a rebellious stage

churchwise. I was smoking and drinking and dancing, which I was raised not to do, so that fit right into my new life. I didn't put a label on it quite. I knew what I felt, and I knew that it seemed to be okay, but queer was the only word I knew and I didn't want to accept that label.

I went back to see this woman in Germany the following year. She was almost forced to make a choice of whether it was going to be a further relationship with me or nothing, and she chose nothing. It was a very unhappy time for me. From there, I came back home and went to college. As far as my own personal life, it was very easy to stay busy and put off making any kind of decision on what kind of life I was going to live.

By age twenty-two, I had met Rose and decided to take the plunge and make a long-term commitment to another woman. When we first started living together, I had a lot of guilt. We met a couple of guys, and I thought, "Maybe I'll go to bed with one of these guys and see if there's anything I've been missing." I just wanted to convince myself that I was doing the right thing. Fortunately, I didn't take that step. We had a real rough time the first couple years we were together.

I've been living with Rose for eleven years, and it's been only in the last year that I have felt good about myself. I've always paid lip service to "Gay is all right. I'm gay and I'm proud." I marched and carried signs and all this good stuff, but it's only been just this last year that I've been really feeling happy and enthusiastic about myself. It's made a whole difference in my life. I'm much more relaxed and I have more energy. One thing that I found very helpful was a lot of reading: feminist reading and books about lesbians. I wish I had done some reading and talked to the right people years ago.

I'm thirty-three years old, and I have one brother. My father's an upholsterer, so I grew up taking apart bus seat cushions. I was born in the Portland area. I've had a couple years of college; I'm an accountant by profession. I'm into bowling and tennis. I love music. I play the piano. I'm so much into politics that I don't even think of it as part of my life, it's just a natural thing I do, like brushing my teeth. Not necessarily partisan politics, but primarily gay rights.

Maria Gonzales

WHAT IS YOUR DEFINITION OF A LESBIAN?

I don't really have a definition of a lesbian, not in the sense of the dictionary. I just love women.

HOW DID YOU REALIZE YOU ARE A LESBIAN?

I didn't realize it, my baby-sitter realized it. She brought me out when I was seven or eight; she was thirteen. One night she started talking about some girls at school who didn't like boys. I said, "What do you mean, they don't like boys?" I was a tomboy, and I really dug playing with my brother and his friends. I didn't understand what she meant, so she started showing me and I really dug it. We had a very heavy sexual relationship for about three years after that.

After she turned me on, I became wild. I started turning on all the little girls my age. There was no big T about it, because of course nobody knew. The baby-sitter knew that there was something wrong about it; I just dug it.

The first time I had knowledge of something being wrong with it was when I was ten, and that was in Georgia. My dad was in the army, so we traveled around a lot. We lived on a farm before we lived on base, and while we were on the farm I met this really nice, nice girl that I fell in love with completely.

I'd be at her house all the time. Her mother thought I was cute, and I'd go to her family reunions. I would trip with her. All of a sudden I went over to her house one day, and they wouldn't open the door for me. My friend said to me later, "You know, my mother doesn't like the idea." I don't remember if it was because her mom found out that I was Puerto Rican, or if it was because I was seducing her daughter. I had been aware of the racial stuff where we lived before, in South Carolina. I'd been called a dirty Puerto Rican or spic. That was very normal, getting in fights and getting beat up and beating somebody up. But at that point, I didn't know if it was the race thing. Then we moved onto base, and I forgot about it.

I'd been called queer and funny all along, but I didn't really relate to that because I didn't talk to anybody about it. The baby-sitter, who had moved to the base in Georgia also, told me what lesbian was. She showed me in the dictionary that lesbian is two women that do it. She said that I was a lesbian. I didn't like being called queer, but I didn't mind being called a lesbian because she was the only one that ever called me that.

The first time it got out about me was when I was thirteen. I got caught by this girl's mother. We were doing it in the back of her station wagon while she was in the commissary. We figured she was going to be in the commissary a long time, so we closed all the curtains around the back of the station wagon. Her mother thought it was the cutest thing she'd ever seen, and she started blabbing it all around the base. It never got to my mother because my mother didn't run in that circle, but it got to all my friends. Everybody knew. It wasn't like I was trying to hide anything; I was just really embarrassed.

I became a cheerleader in the ninth grade, and I did it with three of the girls in the squad. Another girl came up to me and she said, "Did you know that so-and-so is gay?"

I said, "Gay?" She said, "Yeah. She's a queer, a lesbian. She does it with other women. She's done it with X, Y, Z." I said, "Of course, I know. I am, too, stupid. How can you be so blind? Just because I'm on the cheerleading squad?"

The word gay just slipped by. What really got me was queer. And then I realized, "Yeah. I am." I felt all right. I didn't feel bad. I never really got a lot of flak about being that way, I guess. I was lucky. In one sense, I was very accepted: I was a baby butch.

I really related to being a boy. I wanted this machine I could walk into and grow a penis, and then I would be a boy and I could take a girl out. Then I'd walk back into the machine and become a girl again and go home.

I never had a boyfriend, never did it with any boy. When I was in high school, I didn't want to be a boy anymore. I still really wanted women, but I knew that I was a woman. I accepted the fact that I was never going to have a penis, and it didn't matter to me that I wasn't going to have one. I felt good about myself and about being gay.

————————

I was born in Puerto Rico. I'm twenty-nine. My dad was in the navy for twenty years. He still works for the marines in a civilian capacity. My mother works for the marines in a civilian capacity as an office worker. Right now, I'm working with the L.A. Neighborhood Safety Project. They needed a gay Latino to police central L.A. and to bring a bridge of understanding among the gay Latinos, the gay community, and the central L.A. community.

Chrystos

WHAT IS YOUR DEFINITION OF A LESBIAN?
I don't agree with the political definition in which women

say they're lesbians, but they don't sleep with women. But I wouldn't say sleeping with women is the only thing that makes you a lesbian.

I've come to use the words dyke or queer, because I realize that they're saying something about my stance in society. I know a lot of women who think of themselves as gay, or think of themselves as loving women, but that's a very different thing from being a dyke. Somehow, seeing yourself as a dyke is really acknowledging something about yourself. You're not just playing around anymore.

I get a sense that when you're a dyke, that's irreversible. Not too much you can do about it after that. But being gay has a flexibility about it; you can always go back to being straight.

For me, when I really felt like a lesbian was when I began actively making love to other women and wasn't just passive, when relationships with women were more important to me than my relationships with men, when men began to fade out of my life entirely. It took a long time for that to happen, though, after I first came out, because I was really scared.

How did you realize you are a lesbian?

I used to get called a queer in high school all the time, but I didn't know what queers did. I would just get angry and beat up the kids who called me that. I wasn't sure why they were calling me a queer, but they always called me names. Most of the time I'd been sort of an outcast, so it was just another dirty word that somebody was calling me.

My best friend and I were very close. We spent all our time together and wrote letters back and forth during class. It was like a love relationship, but we didn't know what to do, and sex didn't ever come into it, really.

The first time I got attracted to another woman, I was in the nuthouse. She was a technician who was a lesbian, but she was very closety. She snuck me off the hospital grounds a couple times, but I was pretty afraid. We never made love or anything.

I did a lot of things that now, in retrospect, I realize were very lesbian. Like for a joke, one of the women at the nuthouse and I got married in the middle of the plaza and caused a big uproar. We were just doing it to rile people up, we thought. But when I think back on it, it was a pretty weird way to rile people up.

The first woman I slept with was after I ran away from the hospital. She kept calling me a straight girl and wouldn't really deal with me, so that was pretty painful. I figured she was right, that I was just a straight girl who was really confused and that I didn't know what I was doing. I was about eighteen.

Then I came back to the city and got involved with this woman who was into the butch role. I guess my first three relationships were all with women who considered themselves butch, and I was just supposed to be passive and lay back. That was in '65 and '66. Then I got into a relationship that lasted for eight years with Peter, who considered herself the butch, and I was the femme. Even though we lived together all those eight years, I don't feel like I came out as a lesbian during that time, because I'd have one-night stands with men every six or nine months to prove to myself that I wasn't really a queer. I was real uptight about it.

When the Women's Movement started to get known about, I read books like *Sexual Politics* and saw that our relationship had some of the same things that were talked about as being destructive in heterosexual relationships—for instance, the role-playing. I was the dishwasher and she was the money-earner. It was very clear. So I started agitating in the relationship for change. I got into therapy about that time, and I started not to be such a passive person. That went on for about a year, and then the relationship broke up.

When I read *Sappho Was a Right-On Woman*, I came away feeling a lot more like it was all right to be gay, and that's really what I was, and there was no use playing that I wasn't anymore. That was about a year before my relationship with Peter broke up.

I feel like I'm probably atypical of most women who've come out in the sense that I was never particularly accepted the whole time I was growing up because I was not a WASP. So in a sense for me, being gay has just been another part of myself that hasn't fit in with the main world. It couldn't be a very traumatic experience for me because my whole life has been traumatic, and being gay is the one good thing that's ever happened to me. It's been the one transition, or the one way of being that's been comfortable, and that's taken care of me, rather than devastating me.

I've been in a lot of trouble almost all my life, in and out of nuthouses, jails. I was born here in San Francisco. My father was in the civil service, and my mother's always worked as a typist. We were very poor. My family is middle class now because there are no kids at home and my mother's still working and my father has a pension, but when we were growing up they weren't middle class at all. Sometimes it was pretty hard trying to get dinner together.

I don't know anything at all about the Native American side of my relatives because my father has been ashamed of that. I didn't find out until I was about twenty, when my mother told me what his tribe is and where my other relatives were. When I was young, the kids used to call me names, and it was very hard for me to figure out exactly what was going on. So I internalized a lot of that stuff and believed that there was something really wrong with me. I think that was a lot of why, when I got to high school, I was acting out all over the place, getting into trouble, getting into a stealing racket and stuff.

Right now I'm going to San Francisco State. I write poetry and do drawings. Lately, I've been selling a lot of drawings, and that's how I've been making my money. I'm thirty.

Esther Brown

WHAT IS YOUR DEFINITION OF A LESBIAN?

First of all, it's having the desire for companionship and emotional relations with females only. There's no real emotional drive as far as the opposite sex is concerned. Dealing with men if you have to, but avoiding it whenever possible, that's my definition.

HOW DID YOU REALIZE YOU ARE A LESBIAN?

I had a very confused life, really. Coming from the background I did, the socially acceptable standards were you got married, you had a family, and you took care of the male. So I got married as soon as I got out of school. It lasted a very short time, and then I was divorced and went into the service.

Prior to going into the army, I hadn't had any sexual relations with women. I ran around with women almost my entire life, and I had more girlfriends than I did boyfriends, but I'd force myself into dating and getting engaged and getting married because that was the only thing that was acceptable.

Back in Indiana in the forties, a couple of my girlfriends who were real close and were kissing all the time had kind of a lovers' quarrel one night. Well, they were thrown in jail and were going to be interred in a mental institution.

People said, "They're off balance; they're mentally incompetent; they need psychiatric treatment." So the older woman of the two had to agree that she would never see this other woman again. She moved out of town.

With that kind of a background, there was that much more to fight. It wasn't just a matter of saying, "I prefer women, and this is it."

I was in the army two and a half years, and it was while I was in the service that I recognized my lesbianism. I didn't identify it as such at that time; it was just my way of life. There were eight or ten of us on the basketball and softball teams, and when we'd go on trips we'd get a hotel room and flip coins to see who got the room when. All of this stuff was real hush-hush. A couple of our friends got thrown out of the army because they admitted they were homosexuals to the court-martial board. One of them was our athletic officer and the other one was our star softball player, and they got caught in my car. Of course, the officer was allowed to resign, but the enlisted woman was court-martialed.

I recognized my desires to a degree, but I shunned them. I just cast them aside and said, "Well, that can't be." So I got married again. In fact, I've been married four times. Each time, my feelings would be strong in lesbianism, and yet I wasn't strong enough to stand up and say, "Well, I am. Accept it or not. It doesn't change me as a person."

Even prior to the time I was married the fourth time, I lived the life of a lesbian, but it was a closet sort of deal. People might have had their suspicions, but I never came right out and told anyone.

It was a very difficult time in my life. I had relationships with women, and I had lesbian acquaintances. I'd go over to their places for parties, and in a few instances we even went to gay bars. But I had to be very discreet, because when you're in management for an oil company, God knows with the size of that company, no matter where I went in public someone would see me. This was in the fifties and sixties.

At the same time, I went to straight bars; I associated with straight couples. If I went hunting or fishing, I went with straight couples, because I always had this fear for my position. Where you work is a real factor in the time it takes you to come out. I'm sure that's what keeps many, many women from coming out, or from at least admitting it to themselves or anyone else. I'm fifty-three years old, so it took a long time.

It wasn't until the time my last ex-husband came to my apartment and wanted to stay overnight that I finally made the decision: "This is the way I am going to be." He was drunk, just plastered. I told him he shouldn't drive back to Juneau, so he said, "Well, can I sleep with you?" I said, "No, you can't sleep with me." He figured the fact that we'd been married made it perfectly all right.

One thing I will point out—in all these relationships with men, I was never promiscuous. I didn't play the field, male and female. When I felt enough toward a male to get married, thought I could tolerate him, then we'd get married. So even after we'd been divorced, I wasn't about to be promiscuous with him. It was then I decided, "Why play games anymore? I've had it as far as men are concerned." He just put the frosting on the cake when he said, "I'm a man, and you can't do without a man." You know that old story. "I-can't-go-without-sex-I-don't-know-how-you-can-do-without-sex." I said, "Forget it, Sam; go on home. I don't care if you kill yourself." Then's when I decided.

I was born in Muncie, Indiana, in 1923, and I didn't leave the state of Indiana until I went into the service in May of '43. I went to airplane mechanics school, and then I was on an all-WAC line in the army. We had a certain number of planes we were responsible for. That meant that all facets of sustaining those airplanes were conducted by women. We had hydraulic specialists, instrument specialists, radio specialists, and women who did the engine overhaul.

After that, I traveled around and went to New York to the WAC reunion in '46. Then I flew to Alaska and started work for the oil company in May of that year. I worked there until May of '65, then moved down to the ranch here in Washington.

Rose

WHAT IS YOUR DEFINITION OF A LESBIAN?
A woman who loves another woman.

HOW DID YOU REALIZE THAT YOU ARE A LESBIAN?
I always loved women, ever since I was very, very young. That's really true. I never considered men. That's how I became a lesbian. When I was growing up in Italy, I was looking for women. When I was in high school in the States, I was looking for women. I made love to my first girlfriend when I was about eight.

We don't have a word for it in Italian. It was never really brought up, but it just seemed to be live and let live at the time that I was there. Nobody ever talked about it, so I didn't think about whether it was good or bad. You don't grow up with those kind of hang-ups. We might say, "Well, they're strange or weird," or something like that, but we don't use an actual word. I didn't even know there was such a word until I had lived with Jeri for almost two years.

When Jeri and I moved to San Francisco, that's when I started searching it out in Italian dictionaries. I used to go to the libraries a lot, trying to find it, and I couldn't find anything. Then finally I found this one special dictionary that you had to check out at the library; I mean it wasn't even available to you. I looked it up from the English word to the Italian, and it's just the same. We just use the American word, homosexual, but I'd never heard the word lesbian or homosexual, never, until I came to the States.

Personally, I don't feel that a person should go around saying, "I'm gay, I'm gay," because that's a paranoia if I ever heard one. I figure a straight person doesn't come to you and say, "I'm straight." Really, they don't. So why should I have to go up to them and say I'm gay? If they want to think I'm straight, that's their business. If they want to think I'm gay, well, that's their business also. I think everybody's gay, but that's my business because that's where I'm at. I think everyone's gay unless otherwise proven. That's why maybe I'm so comfortable with people.

———————

I'm thirty years old. I came from Italy. I came to the States when I was sixteen. I didn't know any English. I had to go to school and learn English. I was still murdering the English language, and then I took modeling school and I learned how to pronounce my words a little better. My father is a welder, works for a big tractor company that makes huge tractors here in Oregon. My mother, she's a tailor. I have two brothers and a sister. I do accounting work in an office which has about three hundred women.

Canyon Sam

WHAT IS YOUR DEFINITION OF A LESBIAN?

My definition of a lesbian is a woman who is committed to loving other women. I say "who is committed to loving other women" and not just "who loves other women" because I was once with a woman who said she was lesbian, and it turned out she didn't have a real commitment to women. She was still into men, and when things got hard, she didn't have that commitment to work things out. She just split and went off with men.

How did you realize you are a lesbian?

I had a high school friendship with a girl for two years that got pretty intense. We talked to each other every other night on the phone for a couple of hours, and we spent all our weekends together. I had a little flash—"That's not normal. That's not a friendship that you're supposed to have with women." But I didn't get freaked out that I was a lesbian because I didn't think of her sexually.

Months went by, and after you're that close for a year and you aren't able to express it physically, it gets a little frustrating. So then we started being able to touch more, always on my initiative. I thought it was a perfectly natural and perfectly wonderful feeling, and it felt good to her, too. It did freak her out that we'd hold hands or have intense feelings for each other, but we weren't even doing anything heavy-duty. It was just progressing to being able to hug or touch hands. Then towards the end, when things really got intense, we kissed sometimes around the mouth area.

When I would have all these intense feelings after we'd been hugging, it would flash through my mind, "Homosexuals." But then I said, "No, no, that's not what we are because we look perfectly normal. We look like we're out of *Seventeen* magazine. Lesbians wear dark leather jackets and dark pants and boots, and they have real short hair and caps, and they drive trucks, and they have whiskers, and they're real dark and mean. No, that's not me."

In the second year, I felt her starting to pull away. Finally, it came out that she was seeing this guy and that she had been seeing him for months behind my back. I really got pissed and said, "Why didn't you tell me months ago that you were having another main interest? Then at least I would have known to start taking care of myself in other ways." She had been a total main focus in my life. I had a rotten home life and wasn't able to relate in a real way with many people except with her. So afterwards, I was totally devastated. I was seventeen.

I went away to college and continued dating men as I had done in high school sometimes. They were Asian men, and I could relate to them around our common identity as Asians.

After about a year and a half of school, I dropped out and worked with this group of people who were much more open about who they shared loving, emotional, and sexual energy with. Men could be with men, or women could be with women, or women with men. Everything was totally supported. You loved who you loved. It was a person. It could be a man or a woman, but that was just what they happened to be.

There weren't any feminist politics at all. As a matter of fact, there were a couple of women there who identified as lesbians but wouldn't say it because it was too much of an apolitical group. I saw one of them reading *Lesbian Nation* once, and I heard another one say, "I haven't gotten into my own lesbianism yet." I freaked out. That word was just too radical and too extreme. I couldn't identify with it.

I thought those women—just because they mentioned the word—were too heavy-duty for me. That made them dangerous. It was okay if there were women who loved other women, as long as they also loved men. But the lesbians who called themselves lesbians were scary. It was that whole myth of lesbians being after women's asses and being sexual animals. I felt sexually threatened by them.

Later, a woman in the community and I fell in love. We were both naive about having relationships with women, and so we were both scared. We were scared when we were falling in love, and we were scared about being in bed together, and we were scared to really work things out.

We moved in together, and it was wonderful in the beginning. We were very much in love. I was so proud of her I wanted to take her to my family and my parents and all my relatives and say, "Look. This is the one. Isn't she wonderful? Isn't she beautiful?" I felt that if I had been a man and she a woman, I would have wanted to marry her. I really wanted it to be permanent, whatever permanence there is.

We were both so sexually inept and nervous about loving women that it was ridiculous. I was nervous because I was making love for the first time with a woman, and not just any woman but a woman I was totally in love with. When we got in the bed with each other, I couldn't relax. I couldn't feel the feelings. I later found out she really didn't know what she was doing, so she went about it in a very methodical way. But I was so nervous I just felt her doing these things to me, and even though I didn't really feel turned on, I thought it was great. "Oh, gee, we just made love. Wow, this is a consummate experience. It is so wonderful."

In the second week that we were together, she got this new woman friend. One day she said, "I want to sleep with Eve." I said, "We just moved in together, and now it's only two weeks and you're off with someone else? I can't believe that."

I was freaked out, and I didn't have anyone I felt I could turn to. My friends were straight or straight-oriented, and I just didn't trust them with the intense feelings I had for this woman. They would have thought I was weird for feeling so strongly about a woman, when you should just be playing with women and really be into men. So I went to Hawaii and spent a long time being in the country and with myself.

When I came back, I decided to get more into the women's community, so the next time I was in a relationship and something went wrong I would have support. I knew that support could come from women who were committed to loving other women, so I decided just to block off men for a while and get into women. I made a couple of attempts at trying to break into the San Francisco women's community, and they were real failures.

At this time, though, I was also totally weirded-out by the city, so I decided to move to the country. I thought a good launching point would be this country retreat run by women in southern Oregon. I figured they'd probably know if there were other women around.

The night before I was ready to go, they called and said, "We've canceled that retreat." I said, "Well, I just closed up my whole life down here and was preparing to come up." So they said, "Well you can come up anyway and stay over-night, and we can tell you where to go." So that's what I did. I hitchhiked the whole day and spent the night there. Then I went to this piece of women's land where any woman could stay and camp for the summer.

When I got to this isolated piece of land that was out in the boonies, the first thing I saw were these *huge* women. They were tall and big, and they had no shirts on, and they were really into their bodies. They were shoveling or hoeing or gardening.

Then I went into the little hand-built country cabin, and this dark, huge woman came into the doorway. I think she looked much bigger because the doorway was a little smaller than usual, but I just started backing up. I was just going to leave the cabin because I was so totally scared from that first flash. It was the whole stereotype of them being huge, dark-haired, dark-eyed, and dark-skinned. But as soon as she opened her mouth and we started knowing each other, she was very wonderful.

I found out there was this whole community of women in the country. They took me to meetings with them where there were twelve or fifteen women, and I went, "Wow! All these women live out in the sticks, and they're all lesbians, and they have this network with each other."

The word "lesbian" got tossed around a lot. I had always reacted inside and been freaked out by it, but I thought, "It's okay. They can use it for themselves and for each other. It's just that I'm not that. I'm not scared of them, and we like each other, but I'm not one of them. I'm not a lesbian." Right?

I also went into all these trips about defining myself. I couldn't stand putting labels on myself. That's the whole trip of that bisexual phase. If somebody pressed me, I would say, "Bisexual," but otherwise I would say, "Hey, if I fall in love with a person, it doesn't matter if it's a man or a woman; I just go on those feelings." You know, that kind of bullshit. I didn't like to label myself or put what I felt were restrictions on myself, but it also meant I never took a stand for or against anything. The first time I ever allowed myself to be defined was when I called myself a lesbian, and then later a lesbian feminist.

I remember that it felt wonderful when I finally called myself a lesbian. It felt like coming out of a dark cloud and having a lot lifted off me. I could say who I was with pride and not feel like I had to keep down who I was or be ashamed of who I was. I was nineteen.

My parents are Asian, middle class, middlebrow professionals with college educations. They work for the county at civil service jobs. I had a very stable, sheltered, middle class life. I'm twenty-one. I'm interested in the arts, and I've done dance, some theater work, acting, stage managing, concert producing. I'm going to be working on a film. As of now, I earn my income by doing odd jobs—painting, restaurant work. I know a little bit of carpentry, and I might decide to study that as a skill just so that I can always be sure of a job, since I don't have a lot of faith in making money at the arts.

Jane Salter

WHAT IS YOUR DEFINITION OF A LESBIAN?

I guess it's—to catch an old phrase—women loving women. I mean that as an emotional definition: women being in touch with each other in a lot of very deep ways.

HOW DID YOU REALIZE YOU ARE A LESBIAN?

When I was in junior high school, I was in love with my best friend, who was seeing another girl. I was just fascinated by the whole thing, although I was not an active participant. One day in school, they were passing a note to each other about a very sexual dream. That note got picked up, and everybody went into total hysteria.

Everybody's parents were screaming. Everybody was sent to psychiatrists. My mother said I couldn't see my best friend anymore, but I pretended to try and kill myself, so she said I could see my best friend but I couldn't spend the night with her.

Then we all took to dating boys real quickly. My friend ended up being a Nebraska beauty queen, and the other girl got married very quickly and had many kids. I got involved in Jewish Youth Organization, got nominated for Sweetheart, and went out with all these boys. I was supposed to be happy, and I was miserable.

I got to college, and all the girls I met at college had been sexually active for years and years. I felt like an absolute freak. You know, like Sylvia Plath's book dividing the world up into people who'd screwed and people who hadn't. So I kept going out with all these men and going to bed with them and then getting out of bed and leaving in the middle of everything.

Finally, I met a guy at school that I really liked spending time with. We began to live together, and he never touched me. I decided, "This is absurd. Now it's time to really get down to brass tacks." So one night we both dropped mescaline—this was my big plan—so I could seduce him. He said, "You're the only one who doesn't know. You're such an Alice in Wonderland. I'm gay."

In the meantime, I began to realize that a lot of people in my life were gay and that I just hadn't known. I went to work at this place where almost everybody on the staff was gay, and I fell in love with one of the women. I did not know she was gay at first, and I did not think I was gay. I just knew I was in love with her.

Then I met a man and I said, "Well, look. We're going to fuck. I've got to get this over with. There's just something wrong with me." So I invited him over and he spent the night and I wouldn't let him touch me. But he stayed with me six months and we finally screwed, and I hated it. It was just an awful experience. It was the last thing in the world I wanted to do.

Meanwhile, I was seeing this woman. He also liked her very much, and the three of us spent a great deal of time together. It was evident that I was really in love with her and not giving him any time or attention. But she said, "Look, you're living with him. You've been living a straight life. I'm not willing to deal with this." I felt totally rejected.

Then I began to lose my sight. It took about a year to lose it, between the time I was twenty and twenty-one. I stayed with the guy I was living with because it was all a huge change in my life, and it took me a long time to feel secure enough to tell him, "Bye." We never would have lived together so long, otherwise.

I began to be with women while I was living with him.

As a matter of fact, I was hanging out with almost all women, mostly lesbians, but because I was living with this man, I felt that I had no right to say I was a lesbian. I mean, where did that put me? What kind of hogwash was that? But I knew I was. I just didn't know how to explain my position. I didn't want to say, "Because I'm blind I'm insecure, and I'm not ready to live alone yet." I did not want to admit I had that many fears and insecurities about my own life and about all the changes that I was having to make. I felt trapped. I was living the kind of life I didn't want to be living, but I didn't know what else to do.

I started seeing a woman pretty regularly, which got intolerable around here because I couldn't sleep with him at all. Finally, he exploded and said that he wanted to move out, so I got a lesbian roommate for a year, and now I live alone.

I feel like I live in a golden sea. I feel very very rich and very full with the women who live my life with me. I don't have problems getting around because I have so many lesbians in my life. I go swimming every day with different women; and different women take me to all my hospital appointments; and different women help me with my schoolwork; and different women help me with my shopping. It's just like a whole huge family. It's very nice.

I was born in Chicago, and I'm a Taurus with four planets and a moon in Virgo. So I'm very earth-grounded, but my Venus is in Pisces, which makes me absolutely crazy. I moved to Omaha when I was about eleven. I was president of a Jewish Youth Group for Nebraska and Kansas. I did some professional drama and started U.C. Berkeley as a drama major, but I ended up as an English major. I worked at the recreation center for the handicapped here for two years and was going to go into working with the handicapped until I

lost my sight, and then I figured I had to work with the handicapped every day—me, and that was enough. I'm a writer,
and I'm getting a master's in women's literature. I'm twenty-
six. My father has a real estate agency in Omaha, and my
mother teaches anthropology at Nebraska University.

Dolores Rodriguez

WHAT IS YOUR DEFINITION OF A LESBIAN?
My definition of a lesbian is a woman who has chosen to
take a different lifestyle. She can still be a mother; she can
still be a woman; but her sexual attraction, her desire, the
way she's more comfortable is to trip with other women.

HOW DID YOU REALIZE YOU ARE A LESBIAN?
I was very young. I think I started realizing that I was attracted to women when I was seven, or even earlier. My word
was fear. I was sick. I was growing up abnormal. When you're
seven, of course, you're wondering why you're feeling all
these feelings, and you know that you're not supposed to
feel them.

I was going to a Catholic school, and I had two older
brothers who were really on a macho trip. My dad didn't
live with us, and Mom was working or partying, but with
my brothers, the church, and my school, the sexual protec-
tion around me was constant. I was always guarded against
sex, but at the same time I always knew that it was supposed
to be boy-girl or man-woman. When my brothers' girlfriends
would come over, I would stand in the corner and watch
them. I used to get angry and say to myself, "Why can't I
have a girlfriend? Why am I going to have to get stuck with
a boyfriend?" All through my childhood, I was thinking
these thoughts.

I really realized that I was a lesbian when I was eight or

nine and I played with the little girl next door. I said to myself, "I'm a queer. I'm what they always talk about." I had this neighbor, a man everyone used to talk about because he wore thongs and tight pants. I knew he was a queer, that he was trying to be a woman. So I already identified with him.

All through grammar school and high school, I never did try to change. Even though I was tomboyish, to keep up I still went out with guys. I wondered, "Is this just a phase I'm going to grow out of, or is this real?" It wasn't until last year that I said, "This is real." I was walking down the street looking in all these windows. I saw the women dummies in there with the nice clothes, and I wasn't even interested. But if I saw a nice shirt or nice men's shoes, I stopped and looked. That's when I said, "Yeah, I'm a lesbian. I have to accept it. It's not a dream. The reflection in that window is really me. That's how I really look. That's how I really act."

Ever since I was small, I've had visions that a lesbian wore men's clothes and had short hair and had femme girlfriends. Right now, I'm dealing with that, and I'm saying, "Do I really want to play that role?" I see old lesbians with men's shoes and short hair and men's shirts, and I think, "Am I going to go to that extreme, or am I going to break out of it?"

Now I've come to a halt, and I'm saying, "That role-playing was all wrong." But I grew up that way, and it felt all right, until now.

———

I'm twenty-five, and I was born in a barrio in San Diego. My mother's a factory worker, and my real father's in a lettuce camp someplace. My stepfather, he's a farm worker. I saw my mother work her butt off to raise us; I saw the trips she had to go through—her loneliness of not having a man around the house, how it led to her drinking for a while.

I went to junior college in Santa Monica; then I went to Sacramento; then I went to San Francisco; then I landed

here in Los Angeles. Right now, I'm working with GALA
(Gay Latinos) in community affairs, and I have a welding job.

Carol Gay

WHAT IS YOUR DEFINITION OF A LESBIAN?

My definition of a lesbian is a woman who identifies herself as a woman, a woman-identified-woman. That means
she doesn't compare herself to men the way most women do.
She compares herself just to herself and to other women
around her. She relates mostly to women on all levels: physi-
can, spiritual, emotional, psychic, and sexual. When I think
of a lesbian, I think of independent, creative, individual,
strong.

HOW DID YOU REALIZE YOU ARE A LESBIAN?

I grew up in the South where lesbians were not heard of.
I knew what a homosexual was—a man that was sexual with
other men. Mobile was a pretty large gay town for men,
but the lesbian section was small and closeted. "Lesbian"
had no negative connotations because I'd never even heard
the word. In Alabama, "queers" and "fairies" were all men.
To come out in an atmosphere like that was very hard.

I got married when I was seventeen in order to move out
of the house. Nice Southern girls didn't just move into
apartments on their own. Roommates were unheard of. I was
married from seventeen to twenty-two, and the last year I
was married I had a good friend who lived down the street
from me. We would visit every day, and our children would
play together. I remember sitting on the bed talking with
her one afternoon, and I realized I wanted to kiss her. I
didn't want to kiss her like a sister; I wanted to kiss her
passionately. It went through my head perfectly calmly that
I was romantically interested in her and that I really loved

her. It didn't freak me out because I didn't know what a lesbian was, but I knew enough to know it wasn't something I should say to her or something I should impulsively do.

At that time, I had had a couple of affairs with men to test out whether I just wasn't interested in sex or if it was my husband. Finally, I got divorced and continued testing out with men just why my sexual feelings weren't avid.

At one point, I lived with a man who was impotent, which let me out of the sexual thing and gave me what I thought I needed, which was to be in a family unit. At the time, I didn't know why I chose an impotent man, but looking back it's real clear.

His brother's girlfriend, Dee, and I developed a close friendship because we were all living in a big house together, and eventually she and I and my daughter moved into another house by ourselves. She's the woman I had my first lesbian affair with.

I had been thinking that I wanted to make love with Dee before we did it, and I had wondered about it. "Oh, my God, I won't know how. How do you make love to a woman?"

About a month before we actually made love, I had a dream about it. In the very first part of the dream, I said to myself, "I'm real nervous because I don't know what to do." Then I said, "Well, you'll do whatever you want to do. You'll do what comes naturally." At that point, I started making love to her, and it all worked out perfectly. The dream was like, "Here it is. You wanted to know the answer; here's your manual. This is what you do." It took me all through the whole sex act. I woke up feeling fine and *knowing* I wanted to make love with Dee.

When we finally did make love, it happened just because we loved each other a lot, and I didn't connect it to lesbianism. It was a separate unit in my life.

Then I joined the first consciousness-raising group in Mobile. A few months after I joined, the first two lesbian feminists ever to hit Mobile joined it. They said, "We are lesbians. We live together. We've been lovers for five years."

It was a leaderless group, but their influence was definitely felt. They turned us on to books like *Our Bodies Ourselves, Combat in the Erogenous Zone*, and *Memoirs of an Ex-Prom Queen*. Things started connecting in my mind. The more they would say, the more I would think, "Oh, wow. Is this what's going on with me? Is this why I've been wandering around being crazy for the last five years?"

I sometimes wonder where I'd be now if I hadn't run into them. They just made everything fit together. All the things I'd felt but didn't know existed anywhere else except within me were put into words. I had always wondered, "What's wrong with me? It must be me, of course." But in the CR group, I was able to identify with these women who were lesbians and say, "That's the way *I* feel. That's the way I feel constantly. Wow. It's not just me."

That was in 1973. Somewhere along the line enough things fit so that I said, "I am a lesbian." Thinking of myself as a lesbian didn't freak me out. I didn't ever feel like it was a bad thing or that it was something I didn't want to do. It was a relief having it finally fit together.

I am twenty-eight years old. I term myself a lesbian mother with an eleven-year-old daughter. I spent most of my time in the South while I was growing up and while I was married. My mother was a nurse, and my father was a carpenter. I was married for five years; then, after my divorce, I got a degree in journalism. I taught school for a year, and now I work at a gay counseling center in San Francisco.

Vera Freeman

WHAT IS YOUR DEFINITION OF A LESBIAN?
I don't really have a definition. "Lesbian" is something that someone else thought up. I just think when two women are in love, you don't have to give it a name. Lesbianism to me is sharing something together, understanding each other, being able to be yourself and not hiding.

HOW DID YOU REALIZE YOU ARE A LESBIAN?
I fell in love with a young lady when I was between thirteen and fifteen. I knew what I felt, but I didn't know what it was. The guys were calling me a queer. They'd say, "Oh, she won't go out with you, she likes women. She's always with those girls."
Queers to me were guys. I never saw gay women in those days because women kept it well undercover. But I knew what faggots were, and I didn't want to be one of those guys. I guess I figured that's what they were calling me.
In that time, children grew up really dumb to the ways of the world. We were more sheltered. At fifteen, I didn't know as much as my eleven-year-old kid knows about the world out there, because we didn't go anyplace. Contrary to what you may have heard about the way Black people were raised, in those days it was quite sheltered. This was in Milwaukee.
So they convinced me there was something wrong with me and that I should go out with guys. In order to please the guys, in order to stop the noise, I started going out with guys, and I soon forgot my little experiences from the age of nine through fifteen.
I think all little girls experience something like that, so probably you could disregard the nine-year-old thing, but

not the relationship from thirteen through fifteen or the way I felt. That was the same as the way I feel now: the surge, the feeling, the wanting to be with that one person all the time.

Anyway, I immediately decided to change, and I changed. I was always withdrawn, anyway, and it was very easy for me to closet things. Anything not nice got locked away. I got married, and I was married for five years. I had five children, and then I met someone. I found I enjoyed being with her more than I enjoyed being with my husband.

I started reading books on lesbians just because they turned me on. I didn't find many that were very good, and I still felt the societal reaction, "Oh, my goodness. Oh, how could they?" I told my reaction to this woman friend. She said, "You're just reading trash. Let me give you some books that are really good." So she proceeded to give me some books, and I would report to her what I thought of them.

One time I said, "Sure wish I was a mouse peeping out of a hole so I could see what they're doing." She said, "Now, why would you want to see what they're doing?" I said, "Because I want to learn it." I'm sorry I didn't read *Patience and Sarah* about then. I really could have gone about my business much quicker than I did. So through these books, I started to think it was pretty nice.

I also realized that I wanted to be with her more and more. I'd go home and analyze myself, trying to find out why I wanted to be with her. Did I want her to show me something? Did I want to do something with her? And if I did, what could I do? I didn't know what to do. So I confessed to her, "Why do I feel as if I want to do those things that I read in the book? And if I want to, how would I do it?" She said, "Why are you asking me?" I said, "I know you know *that woman*. I'm sure *she's* done it." She said, "Why don't you ask *that woman* if she's doing it? Don't ask me." I said, "Well, she's your friend; you know something. Tell me what she does so that I can do it."

All this didn't happen in one setting. This was over a period of time. It would come up mostly when I was depressed at home—tired of the whole scene, lonely—and she was such a nice person to talk to.

She said she wasn't gay, and she still maintains that she is not. She finally admitted she was bisexual. During the time I knew her, we were lovers. She showed me how to love. But she also tried to talk me into going back to my husband.

She would say, "These things don't last. You'll get over it. This is not what you want. What are you trying to do with your life? What are you doing to yourself? What about your kids?" That always got to me. That always made me tuck tail and run in for a while. There were six-month binges where I wouldn't go out of the house. I wouldn't see women; I wouldn't think about women. Then I would start going crazy, and the only thing that would stop it would be to go and see someone. Then it was like a mad fling for a long time, hiding it, sneaking it. I would wake up again and say, "You've got to stop it. You know you've got to stop it." This was mainly for the kids, because I thought they might get taken away from me.

She never did talk me out of it. I guess I finally realized I was gay when she left. I just liked women. It took from the age of fifteen to at least twenty-seven before I realized that I really was gay, because I hadn't been able to admit it.

I'm from Milwaukee. I was born at the end of the depression. My parents were very poor, but they knew how to farm, so we had chickens, eggs, cheese, butter, milk, and lots of vegetables. It was nice there then. It was pretty, grassy.

I went to schools that had all white teachers who were very kind, who were interested in my learning. I got an education, but I didn't graduate. I got pregnant, had a kid, got married, had several more, and then I finished my education. I'm now a tax auditor. I'm forty-five, and I have eight children.

Mary Howland

WHAT IS YOUR DEFINITION OF A LESBIAN?

A lesbian is a woman who prefers to have her most intimate sexual and emotional contacts with other women, and who generally relates to other women in the same way as you traditionally think of women relating to men.

HOW DID YOU REALIZE YOU ARE A LESBIAN?

For me, it was a long process. I'm forty now. I was the only girl in a family of boys, and I was taught to be the perfect lady. My parents are Fundamental Evangelical, and my upbringing told me to hide everything I was. I was taught that God comes first, the Church comes second, family comes third, and self doesn't come fourth; self doesn't come. To pay attention to yourself, much less to fulfill yourself, was a sin.

I did not know until late in high school, or maybe even college, that there was such a thing as a homosexual. I was very aware that I was interested in women, but the tragedy of the way I was raised was that I honest to God didn't know there were alternatives to *anything*.

I only dated a couple of times in high school, and I dated maybe once or twice each year in college. I really worried about myself, because although I have always liked guys and gotten along well with them, I wasn't interested in them.

I was interested in a fascinated way by the women in the dorm who got into homosexual affairs, but I always panicked and ran the other way. At Nevada U, there were several lesbians in the dorm. I didn't know quite what you called them, but I knew they did something together, and that fascinated but just panicked me. I used to veer around them in the hall, not in disgust so much as I just couldn't handle it.

At bible college, I was on the dorm council. I used to turn in the gals I caught at lights-out time in whatever it was they were doing, and they would get expelled from college. I couldn't identify with them, and yet I was interested.

I bought Bergler's book on homosexuality my freshman or sophomore year of college, but I wasn't able to open it. I couldn't touch it, and I couldn't throw it away or give it away. That book followed me through college, through thirteen years of marriage, and through two more years before I was able to open it.

My senior year in college, I met the man I married. He was the stereotype of the red-blooded American boy. About nine years into our marriage, I started realizing that I didn't want to be married to him anymore, but I wasn't able to think beyond that. When I was putting him through graduate school, I became aware of the fact that I was spending a great deal of time concocting all sorts of fantasies: "What if he doesn't come home tonight? What if he gets killed on the freeway? Then I'll feel good, but I'll have to be guilty, so I'll act guilty." There was always one woman friend or another in my fantasy who comforted me. I still didn't put two and two together.

I did two years of graduate school and got a master's in nursing. It was during those two years that I knew the marriage wouldn't work. I was so repressed I had an ulcer. I was thirty-five years old, and I was everything I had ever been taught to be. I filed for divorce against his will.

When I filed for divorce, I went through about six months of real hell because I was literally reborn. I had never found out who I was. I had never been taught to think for myself. You don't think for yourself. The Church thinks for you, and then your husband thinks for you. It was by far the hardest year of my life, going from being suicidal, severely depressed, and having an ulcer (the last day my ulcer hurt was the day I filed for divorce, by the way) to realizing I am reliable and worthwhile, unfolding every day. Throughout all this time, I also became aware that I was not only personally, but sexually and intimately, attracted to women.

At a friend's home, I met a woman I thought was a lesbian. I mentioned homosexuality in a conversation, and I got no reaction at all from having said the word. What I was trying to do was open up the subject, and it didn't get opened up.

The next day, the woman called me at work. She said, "Okay, Mary, I could really blow my whole life. If you can't handle what I'm going to say to you, you could ruin me." She was a supervisor pretty high up in one of the feed companies. She said, "Last night you really wanted to talk about something. I want to meet you for supper tonight."

We met at a local cafe, sat at a table near the fireplace, and were there for six hours. She said, "Now, I'm a lesbian. You've been indicating several times lately that you want to talk to somebody about it. I just want you to know you can talk to me. I think you're really searching." I said, "Yeah, I want to talk about it because I think I am, but I don't know for sure. I don't know how to tell, but I'm quite sure I am." She said, "Don't rush. Let's spend all the time you want to talking."

She said, "Hold out your hands." I'll never forget this. She took my hands across the table, and she said, "How do you feel?" I said, "I feel fine." She said, "Well, you're holding hands with a lesbian. How does that feel?" I said, "It feels fine, no problem."

Over the next six months, we met a couple of times a month for dinner and talked about how I am and who I am and any questions I had. She shared her life with me. She said, "I've been gay all my life. I've done all the stereotypical things and all the hard things. I would hope to be able to help you avoid some of those things because you're so damn naive and you're so nice. You could really be taken advantage of."

She said, "You know, if you are a lesbian you're going to be meeting people your own age, and most lesbians your age have come up the hard way. You've come up the beautiful way. You're going to have a hell of a time finding someone your own age who's going to be able to relate to you. You've been in stable relationships. You're a positive person. You're a warm, open, giving human being, and most lesbians your age have learned—because of what they've experienced—to be tough and closed and to take instead of give."

Many months after our talks, I drove in from my small town to visit a friend in Minneapolis, who was a lesbian. We went out to dinner together, and when we got back it was cold and raining and too late to drive fifty miles back home, so I spent the night at her house. One thing led to another, and she said, "I'm having a hard time sleeping because I'm really attracted to you. I know you've been toying with the idea. I really care about you as a friend, and I don't want to do anything to hurt you. I don't love you, I'm not in love with you, but I can't sleep because I'm so turned on." I said, "Well, let's do it. I'm not afraid, and I'd love to have an experience." We did, and it was beautiful, and I was not afraid. This woman was just scared to death for months afterward because she, too, was a time-hardened lesbian, and she kept checking out with me, "Are you okay?" I said, "Yeah, I'm fine."

The experience with the woman that night told me that that was where it was at for me. I had suspected it, but I'd never had an intimate experience with a woman. It was not that anything happened that was so different, and I wasn't in love with this person, but it was just fantastic. It was a hundred times better than anything my husband and I had done together, and the only good thing in our thirteen years of marriage had been the sex life. We had had a good sex life.

Then I knew I was a lesbian. The next day, I was sitting in my apartment in this small town, thinking, "I should feel guilty and I'm not!" I felt so good. I felt as if the final piece had fallen into place.

I was born April 12, 1936, in Boston. When I was eight years old, we moved to Nevada. My father's an appliance repairman, and he retired last year. My mother is a house-wife who never worked outside of the home. When I was eighteen, I came to Minnesota to go to bible college and have lived here ever since. In my present job, I am the head nurse of a large convalescent hospital.

Olivia Moreno

WHAT IS YOUR DEFINITION OF A LESBIAN?

Anyone who considers herself a lesbian, I consider one. I don't believe in labels very much.

HOW DID YOU REALIZE YOU ARE A LESBIAN?

I have eight brothers, so I didn't think it was strange when I was little that I had crushes on girls because all my brothers did. It didn't dawn on me that it was wrong until I was in the sixth or seventh grade, when I remarked to my mother one day that I really liked this chick. She said, "Well, if you feel that way there's nothing I can do about it, but maybe you shouldn't talk about it in public." She didn't get down on me personally; she just said that society wouldn't be able to accept it.

When I was fifteen or sixteen, I read *Lesbian Woman*, by Del Martin and Phyllis Lyon. Then I knew what I was, and it got to be bad. I hid the book under my mattress. When I had a label for myself and knew there were really people like that and knew people didn't like people like that, then I started going into the closet really strong.

Last summer when I was sixteen and seventeen, I went to college here in Olympia, and I had the first real relationship I've ever had. I knew what I was. It made me feel weird, but that's the way I was so I was going to have to accept it. I didn't tell anybody else.

I really came out this summer at college. I figured that if I did anything before I was eighteen, I was illegal, so I waited until I was eighteen. I walked into the Gay People's Alliance and talked to the director, who gave me Gay Youth as a reference. I called up the spokesperson for Gay Youth, and they made my coming out easy.

So it's just in the last four months that I've called myself a lesbian. I knew I was, and I'd say, "I'm gay," or, "I'm weird." I used all different terms except lesbian for myself because it was so socially unacceptable. But now I can say it. I've realized that this is what I am, and I don't want to live a lie. People are going to have to accept me the way I am, and if they don't want to, then it's their problem.

I just turned eighteen. I was born in Cathlamet, Washington. I went to school in Cathlamet until I was fourteen, moved to Cincinnati to be with my dad for five months, then moved back to Cathlamet. Now I go to college, and eventually I want to get my Ph.D. in Adlerian psychology. My mother's been married and divorced four times. My dad's a

Mexican and my mom's white, but I tell everybody I'm a
Chicana. Because of my last name, people assume it anyway.

Jacqueline Denton

WHAT IS YOUR DEFINITION OF A LESBIAN?
A woman loving another woman.

HOW DID YOU REALIZE YOU ARE A LESBIAN?
When I was attracted to Sandra just this last summer, I
felt very strongly that this was where my feelings were. After
recognizing my feelings for Sandra, I went back into my
memories and found lots and lots of hints of it before.

One simple one is that I've always been extremely attracted to women's figures and beauty. I've often said to a
woman that I was shopping with, "Look at that absolutely
gorgeous figure." She'd say, "Oh, Jackie, what are you saying
that for?"

I was a tomboy when I was at school. I definitely wanted to
be a boy, and I wore knickers around 1912 when no little
girls wore knickers. I thought of myself as a cowboy for a
stretch of time, but that's fairly normal. Naturally, many
girls want to be boys because boys get so many goodies.

Then there was one episode when I was finally making up
my mind to get a divorce. I became very much attached to a
young woman who was working in the same agency I was.
This would have been in 1926. That relationship lasted
about a year. It was very supportive for me because I was so
miserable and having such a dreadful time with the divorce,
and I think I used her. She became deeply dependent on me,
and that scared me, so I really closed it off. I've only looked
back on it just recently and not been very pleased with how
I conducted myself.

I know how strong my feelings were at the time, but I never even thought of the word lesbian. It was almost as if it weren't a current word. I just thought we loved each other and wanted to be together a lot, although I also saw it as something that should be kept hidden. Even though close relationships between women were awfully common at that time, and two women might be deeply fond of each other, with us there was a physical love relationship as well. Women could live together, have long-lasting close friendships, and nobody would say anything about it because in the first part of the century it was still perfectly acceptable. I think they used to call it a Boston Marriage.

So, that was in my background but long since discarded. After that, in the mid-fifties, I had a very marvelous two-year love affair with a man who had been in love with me for many years. I'd known him in college. After he died of cancer, it was as if there wasn't going to be any relationship that would take its place. I didn't want to live alone, but I was going to be very, very choosy about the man I would have anything to do with.

What happened, of course, was that I was always a little bit looking out for somebody. I was looking for a man, distinctly. When I retired and came to Cambridge to live in 1970, I found myself having a wonderful time with a wide variety of friends, but hardly anybody of my own age.

Then I went through a period of considerable restlessness, and I was reading a lot of feminist books. The idea of a lesbian relationship began to make me think, "Hey, this is probably what is going to be right for me." One of the books I was reading was *Women and Madness*. That book made me good and angry. It was about the mistreatment of women and how the psychiatrists and everybody else have been fucking us up. There were also considerable accounts of the situations of lesbians, both with regard to psychiatry and with regard to the quality of their lives. Again, an echo was coming into my life that this was a possibility.

A year ago, an eighteen-year-old college student was sent to me for counseling. She was gay, and she talked with me quite a lot about being gay and about her relationship with her lover. It seemed perfectly okay to me in every way.

I had some definite feelings toward women, too. I am in three women's support groups. In the older women's group, I had a very definite feeling one time that I would like to be close to one of the women. I know her very well, and she and I are just generally fond of each other. I had little feelings that maybe something could develop there for me—a relationship that would be more loving than just friendly. I never made any moves, and neither did she. In one of the other groups, there was a younger woman for whom I felt some considerable attraction but realized that that wasn't what I wanted; she was in pretty desperate need of constant support about one problem, and that didn't feel good to me.

So, that's the past history of little hints. One thing after another came along, particularly my dissatisfaction with men.

Then, one time, Mandy—who's a member of the second support group and who is a lesbian—said to me, "You ought to come out for practice on our softball team." I said, "Sure, I'd love to," laughing like crazy because I don't play softball. I mean, I had played a few times in my life, but I always closed my eyes when the ball came toward me (I don't anymore). I said, "When?" She said, "Sunday." I said, "Oh, I can't this Sunday. It's too bad, but I promised to go to something else." She said, "Well, can't you get away from this particular thing and come over to my house afterwards?" I said, "Sure. Anything special?" She said, "Well, one of the people on the team has been talking about how interested she is in older women." I said, "Well, well."

So I went to Mandy's house, and we all drank beer and told stories. Sandra stayed on afterwards and I could pay more attention to her, but I wasn't sure she was the one Mandy had mentioned over the telephone. The next step was just delicious. Mandy said to me, "Sandra wants to know how you feel." "Well," said I, "I'm not disinterested."

So then Sandra and I had a couple of dates, and things really began to move. We've been together two and a fraction months now. It's a great big fat lifetime to me. It's remarkable to me that she doesn't pay any attention to the difference in age. I'm seventy-two and she's thirty-two, and, of course, she's done tremendous things for me.

If I had come to this conference in California without knowing Sandra, I would have been anxious about practically every contact with an eligible man. Would it turn out to be something? Of course, he's going to be married. Of course, he's going to be attached, and so forth. All the time I would have had one eye out—what's he like? That's not a nice thing to admit, but it's so; I don't want to live alone, and I'm very much in need of love.

But now it's as if I'm not so hungry. I have the feeling that here is a world that will nourish me. If Sandra goes on to somebody else (don't say it), there will be other women I can find. So I don't feel so isolated. At least two lesbians came on to me here at the conference, which was wonderful and very reassuring.

And so when you said did I think of myself as a lesbian, I said, "What else am I going to call myself?" I'm fresh out of the egg, but I'm a lesbian.

My family was fairly well-to-do, and I had a good education. I went to Antioch College for three years, and then I went to Smith for very adolescent reasons: I was engaged to an older man who thought I should be at Smith.

After I graduated, I immediately married a very prominent Princeton man. I discovered fairly soon that things weren't rosy in the marriage, but I wanted to have children, and so I did. I had three children. Meanwhile, of course, in all of those seventeen years of marriage, I was the one who had to make it be a good marriage. We were really taught that if the woman did her part right, everything would be lovely. So it took some doing to finally release myself from that marriage.

After the divorce, I went to work in a coeducational boarding school in Maine. Just being involved with a coeducational boarding school was pretty radical at that time. The funny thing was that parents didn't hesitate to send their daughters there, but they didn't want to send their sons because their sons might get contaminated by the women.

It was a wonderful life for me there. I was a secretary first, then taught art, and then, added to the art teaching, I was treasurer of the school finances. When I retired, I chose to live in Cambridge because that's where the action is.

I started going to women's groups three years ago, and that opened up my life a lot. I'm really into the whole principles and practice of feminist therapy. I've only had a very few clients in counseling, and I'm not so sure I want to do it yet. I have a very good life, and I've been traveling a lot. I'm a lucky bastard, is what I am. Family money and no worries. The business with Sandra is good luck enough. I'm seventy-two.

Dealing with the World Around Us

The rest of the book is organized so that it can be used as a handbook or reference. While only you can determine when, how, or whether to "come out" to the people around you, hopefully these next sections will give you a springboard of ideas for creating the lifestyle that best suits you.

If the decision facing you is whether or not to tell your family, children, or minister, simply turn to the chapter covering that subject, and there you will find a variety of possible ways to deal with the situation. Similarly, if an employee or client has told you she's a lesbian, or if you would like to be prepared in case someone should tell you she's a lesbian, again, you can read how a number of lesbians have felt when telling a boss, therapist, or parent.

When I interviewed the women, I encouraged them to

focus on whatever topics were most important to them. Some had no problems with certain areas and either omitted them or only addressed them briefly. I decided to include all the responses, however, because to include only those that discuss problems would distort the pictures of our lives. We vary greatly as to what areas of our lives have been troublesome and what areas joyous.

Bon voyage.

Within Our Families
Parents and Siblings

Deciding whether or not to tell your parents, how to tell your parents, or how to keep it from them is often a big concern once you have accepted your identity as a lesbian. How will telling or not telling your parents affect your relationship with them? How will telling or not telling them affect the way you live your life? How much time and energy are you willing to put into keeping it from them or dealing with their reactions? All the women you have met so far had a lot to say about this decision and its consequences except Jackie, whose parents were dead when she realized she was a lesbian.

In this section, you will meet Carol Queen's parents and Olivia Moreno's mother. You will also meet three new women, Tonya, Jesse, and Kathy, and their mothers. Since part of the process of figuring out "how to say it" is often imagining what your parents' reactions will be, I have included a few parents so they themselves can relate how it felt to be told or to find out that their daughters are lesbians. Again, this small sampling doesn't begin to demonstrate the variety of feelings parents may have.

Closely tied to the decision of telling your parents is deciding whether or not to tell sisters and brothers. Can you tell some family members and not others? Who should know first? Here you will meet Carol Queen's brother, John, and Kathy's sister, Shelly, who will share their reactions with you.

Again, Jackie had little to say about her siblings: "I wouldn't tell either my sister or my brother directly. My brother's straight and intolerant, and my sister is neurotic. If they should happen to see me in a Gay Pride March they'd just think, 'Oh, that's Jackie being crazy again.' They would think I was supporting friends or something."

Carol Queen

After I took the gay studies class, I joined a bisexual women's rap group, and they gave me a lot of support for telling my parents. I decided, "Well, since I'm gay, I'd better tell them." I really did want to establish some kind of rapport with them on that side of me. There were not a whole lot of sides of me where we had established rapport at that point, so I figured, "I don't have very much to lose, but I have a lot to gain." Someplace inside me I knew that if my family was supportive, I had won a big victory.

I went home from college for the summer and planned. At the beginning of every week, I'd thought up a new master plan and had scrapped it by the end of the week. I was really nervous. "How do I approach them? Go in when they're watching 'Password' and say, 'Turn off the TV, Mom and Dad, and guess what?'"

Then the problem got solved for me. Two of the women from my gay studies class were going to get married that July in Eugene, and I wanted to go, but that would involve a bus trip. I went in to Dad, who was reading the paper, and said, "Dad, can I go to Eugene this weekend?" He could have just said, "Okay, go. Collect enough pop bottles, get your own bus fare." I wouldn't have cared, I would have done dishes. But he said, "What do you want to go to Eugene for?" I said, "Well, I've been invited to a wedding." I thought that was safe. It sounded all right to him, too. He said, "Oh, whose wedding?" I said, "A friend of mine in a class; her name is Jill." And he said, "That sounds nice. What class?" It was the eleventh hour; I knew it. Either I had to lie my way out of it and then go back and cover up my tracks later, or say it; so I said, "Gay studies."

He was reading his paper, and he just crumpled it up and said, "Jesus Christ!" I said, "Dad, relax." He said, "What are you in a class called gay studies for? I'm sending you up there to get an education."

I said, "Well, I feel I have a large interest in the subject of homosexuality. I have a lot of gay friends, and I thought that I would see what was going on. I got credit for the class, Dad."

He said, "Oh, well, who is she marrying?" I said, "Helen." He smashed the paper together worse this time and said, "Oh, Jesus Christ, I suppose this means you're a homosexual." I said, "Well, I guess you could say that. Actually, I'm a bisexual, Dad, but if you want to think of it in those terms, you're perfectly welcome to." He said, "Oh, Jesus Christ. What does this mean? What does this all mean? All the troubles I'm having here at home and you tell me this."

He went through a classic, "Oh, why are you doing this to me?" scene, except that I have a good enough relationship with my father so that I could say, "Hold on. You're over-doing it. I've just told you something about me that's a very

essential fact, and I want you to be able to take it seriously
and calmly."

He said, "Well, goddamn it, I raised you so that you would
have an interest in the world, and I thought that you were
going to go out and be something important and change the
world and become a lawyer or a newspaper correspondent,
and here you tell me that you're a homosexual."

I said, "I could still be a lawyer or a newspaper correspondent, Dad. I mean, it's not a full-time vocation."

He said, "Goddamn it, I don't see how having an overriding interest in homosexuality is going to solve the problems of the world." I said, "Can you tell me one thing that's
going to solve all the problems of the world? I think that
having an overriding interest in one thing that is a social
problem and a big social phenomenon, and trying to deal
with that in as rational a way as I can, is going to do a lot
more than going out and being a second-rate correspondent
on the *Register Guard*, for instance." I challenged him to
tell me how I should solve all the problems of the world,
and he couldn't think of a way, so he had to back down.

But he said, "Well, don't tell your mother." I understand
that that's a real classic line among parents of gay people.
"Don't tell your mother, don't tell your father, don't tell
your grandparents, don't tell anybody else. I can deal with
it, but nobody else can." I said, "Okay, you tell her. Whatever. Can I go to Jill and Helen's wedding?" He grumblingly
said, "Oh, go to Eugene, go ahead, I don't care. Jump off a
bridge, I don't care."

I went to the wedding, which was really nice, and when
I came back, he sort of avoided me for a week. Then one day
he came up to my room and said, "You know, I don't understand what you told me, but I'm glad you told me." I said,
"Well, I'm glad you feel that way."

And then, after about a week of lull, he became practically
the most pro-gay person that I have ever met. Apparently,

he had thought about it and decided, "Well, I love my daughter. My daughter is gay. Therefore, being gay can't be all bad, if it's bad at all."

After that, he had all kinds of questions. He wanted to know what gay people did, and I told him. I said, "You want to know about men?" He said, "Sure, I guess so." I said, "Well, kissing, touching, fondling, holding each other, hugging, mutual masturbation, fellatio, and anal intercourse. I don't know anything else because I'm not a man so if they do anything else, I couldn't tell you."

He said, "That's enough; how about women?" I said, "The same thing, with the obvious exception that they don't have a penis to do any of the penetrating stuff with. Mostly, it's a very sensual kind of lovemaking."

We would spend a lot of time together in the evenings, and every once in a while he would just pop up out of the blue with a question like, "Hey, do you remember Miss So-and-so who used to be a teacher with me at such-and-so school district? Is she a lesbian?" I said, "Well, since I haven't seen her since I was eleven years old, I couldn't tell you for sure, Dad, but I suspect she is because she lived with the same woman for twenty years, and they moved from place to place together and seemed to have a real cozy little household." He said, "Yeah, I always wondered about that. I didn't think it was my business to ask them, though." I said, "That's very true. They probably would have freaked out if you had asked them back in those days."

Then he wanted to know about five of my friends, all the gay people that I had ever introduced him to. And I said, "Yeah. You're right; they are." He said, "I've been wondering about Paul, too. How about Paul?" I said, "Paul? I never thought of it." Since he had batted a thousand up to that point, I thought that I had better go and talk to Paul. Sure enough, Paul's gay. I thought, "Boy, my father must have insight like crazy!"

Some of my funniest anecdotes are about my father. One day he went into the Glide bloodmobile, stuck his arm out to the lady, and said, "My daughter's a lesbian." I'm surprised she didn't stab him with the needle and go through his bone.

She said, "Do you know what the Bible says about that?" He said, "No, and I don't want to know. I love my daughter and I think she's fine the way she is, and the Bible probably says that she's not, so I don't want to know."

When I heard about that, I thought, "I should give this guy a button to wear; he'd be great." He clips out little things in the newspaper and sends them to me, like "Gay Rights in Sweden Has Won a New Victory."

We still have all the father/daughter conflicts and hassles that go on and that always went on, but on that one level we're secure.

At the beginning of this year, the gay community decided to approach the city council again to get a citywide anti-discrimination ordinance passed. I was definitely interested in working with that, so I said, "Dad, how would you feel about my being in the paper?" He said, "Well, I don't know how your mother's going to take this, but she'd better know." I said, "Okay, what do you think we should tell her?"

I let him set the stage, and he went home and said, "Bernice, Carol has something to tell you. She's going to be up later, and we'll all talk." Mother didn't know what was going on, the poor woman.

I don't even remember what I said to my mother, but she was calm as anything. She said, "I'd be a lot more upset if you came home and told me you were pregnant." I said, "Well, the chances of that are decreasing every day."

It turned out that Mother asked all the same questions that Dad had asked, except what gay people do in bed, which she didn't want to know. She said, "You remember

Miss What's-her-name that Dad used to work with, was she a lesbian?" I said, "We've been through this, and yes, she's a lesbian." She also asked some interesting sociological questions. She'd read an article in *Time*, and we talked for two and a half hours, at least, just having a neat conversation. Then she said, "Whatever you want to do is fine with me, as long as you're happy."

So it seldom comes up anymore. Mother comes to Gay Youth meetings on occasion, and everybody calls her Mom, and she loves it.

My little brother was the first person in my family that I told. He just looked up at me and said, "Oh, well, there's a heartache in every family," and went back to what he was doing. He's two years younger than I am; he'll turn eighteen pretty soon. This was when he was about fifteen. It was just funny.

William Queen

HOW DID YOU LEARN THAT YOUR DAUGHTER IS A LESBIAN?

I asked her. When she first went to the university, one of the things that bugged me all year was that she didn't come home and visit us more often. I've read since that this is a natural pattern, but I didn't know it at the time. Also, she told us in letters that she was going to some kind of a women's group, and after third term at the university, when her grades came there was a gay course on there. I still didn't catch on.

Then, one time, she wanted to go to a wedding in Eugene, and when I asked her who was being married, she gave me the names of two girls. I don't recall exactly how we got into the discussion—maybe it was the time she told me about the wedding—but anyway, we were sitting around the living room having some kind of conversation, and I said, "So I

guess I'm to assume that you're gay, then." And she said,
"Yeah."

It wasn't really any big surprise to me because I had had
too many clues. If you're hanging around with the gay community, you've got to be gay, don't you? I'm not very smart,
but I'm not completely dumb.

Now, you must understand that people who grew up in
the thirties don't know anything about the gay community.
I'm fifty-four years old, I spent four years in the army, and
I don't know that I have ever been approached by a gay
person. Lots of people I talk to have, in one place or another.
But this has never happened to me, so I didn't know anything about the gay community except from the headlines
in the paper, and those come mostly out of New York or
San Francisco.

I asked Carol at the time she told me she was gay, "Did
the fact that you were able to read anything you wanted
to read all your life have anything to do with your being
gay?" She said, "No. It just made it easier for me to find out
what this different feeling was." I think she mentioned it
was during the fifth grade or so that she knew she was different in some way.

So I don't know that it upset me. What could I do about
it? I know now that you can't do anything about it, but even
at the time, I never thought in terms of getting medical help
for her or something like that, because you don't tell Carol
what to do. And I know at this point if I had made any
stink about it, I would have lost her completely. And I think
that Carol's just a little more important than that.

I did tell her, "Let's wait for a while to tell your mother,"
because Bernice was going through some problems at the
time. And so we sat down here one night and told her
mother, and she never got that upset about it. That's been
one of the really surprising things to me, because her mother
comes from a Northern European background, and her whole

idea of sex is not as out in the open as some nationalities.

I told one young couple who are probably about thirty years old, and they said, "Oh, it's probably just a phase that she's going through." They were a little bit shocked.

And I told the principal of the school where I teach, just to let him know what was on my mind. He knew other things were on my mind, and he's a man I can trust. I also showed him the article the other day when Carol's picture was in the paper. I said, "I just want you to know this, just in case." His reaction was mainly, "There isn't anything you can do about it. Things outside of what you can control, you might as well accept."

I also told the lady I eat with, who is seventy-two years old. I showed her the article, and she said, "Boy, you've got a lot on your mind, haven't you?"

I haven't heard a thing about it at school. I'm sure there must be a few people who take the paper, but I haven't heard a word.

Carol told us a long time ago that sooner or later she'd get in the newspaper. She said, "I'll be the spokesman sooner or later, so just get ready to handle it however you're going to handle it." So this thing in the paper wasn't that big a surprise.

I will tell you something else that's ironic about this whole thing. I have recognized for a long time, and I suppose everybody has, that there are a lot of things wrong with our country. And really all I wanted for both my kids was that they do something to make this country a better place to live. Of course, I was thinking of it in terms of being a lawyer and fighting for the downtrodden. This other thing never entered my mind. But maybe what she does will make this a better world for those people who are gay. It has occurred to me, in a way I had never thought about during all those years, that perhaps I will have had my wish when I get old and ready to die.

I think that the time will come when everybody will accept homosexuality. One of the persons that I told about the newspaper article was a country girl who said, "Oh, Christ, if this had happened ten years ago, you'd have really had problems, but I don't think anything will come of it." This summer, when I told my uncle who lives in California, he said, "Aw, nobody pays any attention to that anymore."

I just love Carol. I think she's a neat person. She's been in the Gay Liberation Movement since it started; she carried the arguments in the school for it. And I think that anybody who accepts the fact that young people have ideas and should have a chance to express them would like her.

If what I have said helps some other father or mother— who suspects that they have a gay child—to open up the doors themselves so that they can go ahead and love that person for the rest of their lives, then I think that your book will have been very useful. Living without the love of the children you brought into the world must not be a very good way to live, I suspect. I suspect it would break some people's hearts.

I look at the thing this way. I could have lost my daughter to drugs, to destructive political activism, to any number of things. I could have lost her and not had her anymore in my life. If I had been bullheaded and said, "No daughter of mine is going to be like that," I really could have lost her. No different than if she had been in a car wreck. I don't think being gay is all that big a thing.

Bernice Queen

HOW DID YOU LEARN THAT YOUR DAUGHTER IS A LESBIAN?
She told me about a year ago around Thanksgiving time.

She had told my husband before me, and he said she should hang off and wait a bit before telling me.

One day she came in and she said, "I just want to tell you something, Mother; I'm gay." I said, "Much better that than pregnant." I sincerely felt that. I love Carol very much, and if this was to be her lifestyle, I knew that I was going to have to learn to accept it. I wasn't overreacting in any degree that I can remember.

My thinking up until that point had been what the stereotype has been. I lived in Washington, D.C., during World War II, and I heard about them, but there wasn't a soul that I've ever known in my life that I knew was. Anything that I'd ever read before had always been negative. So the only reason that I'm tolerant is because it's our daughter. This is giving me the first awakening. Now my mind's opened up considerably, having had exposure to her and the things she's concerned with.

I didn't really suspect anything before she told me. My husband mentioned one time a friend of Carol's whose family didn't relish the idea of their daughter coming home for Christmas. I said to him, "I can't imagine any girl who could do something so terrible that her family wouldn't want her home for Christmas." He said, "I'm sure glad you said that." Apparently Carol had already told him. So I got a little tiny inkling at that point, although I didn't have anything to base it on, really.

After she told us, then I called all my close friends in and around the Eugene area and told them. Carol had said to me, "Maybe I'll get up in front of the county commissioner someday or be on the news some night, and I don't want you to be shocked." So when her picture was in the paper a week ago, all these people I care for had already been notified.

I'm working for good friends I've known for years, and it's a good thing I told them because they get the paper, and they saw Carol's picture. It was a lot easier for me to go to work the following Monday knowing that they already knew. So it hasn't been any earthshaking thing, as far as I'm concerned. One good friend said, "Well, there goes Carol, crusading again." I don't think it's the smartest thing in the world, but if she's going to be gung-ho, she has to be honest with herself. This is the way I see it. It's Carol, it's her decision, and even if she steps on our toes a little bit, that can't be helped. And if she turns out being able to do some good, all the more power to her. Let's hope she does.

After Carol's picture was in the paper, I had one phone call that sounded like a teenager. He said, "How do you like having a lesbian for a daughter, bitch?" and I hung up the phone. I thought as I hung up, "Oh, that was stupid. Why wasn't I quick enough to say, 'Much better than having her with a bigot like you'?"

Four or five months ago, a store that was run by lesbians had its window broken. So I called the women up and told them I sympathized with them, that I realized they were being harassed. I told them who I was, and I told them about Carol, but they were older, so they didn't know who Carol was because she's with the Youth Group.

I think Carol and I are closer now that she's told me, because she is able to be more honest with me. She doesn't have to hide this. Now, any time she has a meeting or talks to the attorney, she'll come and tell me about it. But if she hadn't told me, she'd have to keep all this on the inside. It's better that I know.

When she told some of the young people that she was going to tell us, they just about had a fit. "Don't. Don't. They'll never forgive you." But Carol says, "I think I know my mother and dad better than that." And if it's a matter of losing her or not losing her, I'll accept it. It's just that simple in my mind.

John Queen

HOW DID YOU LEARN THAT YOUR SISTER IS A LESBIAN?

I really don't remember. I think it was a dawning awareness; then she probably told me. It was several years ago. I didn't mind, one way or the other. It's nothing to me.

With my particular last name, the kids pick up at a remarkably early age that you can change just the one letter, and there you have "queer." I'd been called queer for years on no particular basis, and so I figured that if all these people said homosexuality was wrong, they were probably wrong, and that there was really nothing to it, one way or the other. I never really received that much bad press about homosexuality, and when I did, the people putting it down could never give me any reason why. The best they could do was that it was immoral, and I figured that I should be able to decide for myself what is and isn't harmful.

I go to all the Gay Youth meetings just to see how much interest there really is in becoming an informing organization to the rest of the community. People don't know that, when you come right down to it, there really isn't anything wrong with it. They're not perverts. Well, maybe a couple. No one's going to come up and accost you or anything. I figure that if you don't know how to turn down a sexual proposition, then you're going to be occupied an awful lot.

Most of the people there assume that I am gay. I don't think something that private and that personal is really a topic of discussion. When people ask me, I tell them, "Sort of, not really. I'm basically asexual, not sexual." But that sounds like a physical problem. It just wouldn't be the right thing for me right now.

Unless a friend brings up the subject and really presses

it, I don't discuss it. It's not really anybody's business what I do or what anybody in my family does. In most cases, a revelation about Carol would be more negative than positive, because then it's guilt by association. If your sister's one, then you can't say you're not one and have someone who thinks it's bad believe you. Some people think it runs in families. I don't tell people unless I think it will sit right with them. I don't feel it's necessary to alienate someone who would otherwise be my friend because of one particular view that they hold. It wouldn't do anybody any good.

Laverne Jefferson

When my older sister found out I was gay, she just flipped. This was the sister who had made me go to bed with her when I was six. She read my letters at home when my lover and I were staying with a lady in Tucson, and she wrote the lady there and said, "Laverne and them are homosexuals." The lady goes, "I know it; I hear them all the time at night." Of course, me and the lady had gone to bed one night already, so she didn't say too much.

My sister ran around and told everybody, "Oh, Laverne's a homosexual." I thought, "Wow, what's going to happen now?"

My father said, "I heard some talk." I said, "Yeah? What kind of talk?" And he wouldn't say it. He goes, "I don't care what people say. I still love you. You're my baby daughter and I always will." And that was it.

My mom still can't accept it. She pretends she does, but every once in a while when she gets drunk I hear her telling somebody. It don't be very pretty when she says it. She calls me a whore. She says "queers" or "faggots." See, that's the Black culture. They're just different. She can't deal with it.

She always tries to say, "Where's your boyfriend?" And I say, "I don't want no man." And then she gets upset again.

There's ten of us kids in the family. They all know I'm gay because my sister told them, too. At one time, all my brothers tried to get my girlfriend, but that didn't work. They wouldn't try it forcefully, but they'd say, "Hey, I've been looking for you." They finally got over that.

Our family grew up so distant that we don't communicate at all, and that makes it really hard. If one of us is in trouble, we get them out of trouble, but we don't talk about it. I see them all the time. We get loaded together and we talk shit.

My oldest brother accepts me. He's a trip. He comes back from San Francisco and he goes, "Yeah, I seen these two guys; I seen all kinds of gay people." My mom says, "What?" He goes, "They're all *people*." I think he had gay tendencies at one time. My brothers are down on me, but I know all about them doing their little things, too. Shit.

Jeri

My parents were very strong Christian people, and knowing how strictly they adhered to the Bible teachings, I never felt comfortable talking about it with them. For the first couple years, Rose and I tried having two bedrooms and making it known: "This is my room." My mother would say, "How come there's hardly any clothes in your closet? How come she's got the nicer bedroom?" I always appeared to have the tacky bedroom. After a couple years, we quit playing that game, and I never tried to hide anything from them except books. They'd come to visit, and it was very obvious Rose and I slept in the same room.

My mother was always very fond of Rose. She said, "I

always wanted a daughter with brown eyes, and now I've got her." Many times I have thought my family liked Rose better than they liked me. My grandma always asks about Rose but never about me, which makes me a little paranoid, but that's my grandma.

Rose and I didn't live in the same area as my parents for a long time, so we were pretty free. We had a picture of us on the front page of the *Chronicle* one time with a caption that said, "Gay Marriage Boom." Of course, it was the typical back-of-your head thing, so it wasn't too obvious. We did get married, but after that article.

We moved back here to Portland when my mother was sick with cancer. She died five months after we got here, so I never really had to deal with telling her. To be perfectly honest, I'm not sure I would be at the stage of development I'm at now if she were alive. That's kind of a strange thing to say because I would love to have her back, naturally. It's just that I felt very close to my mother, and I think I would probably still feel it would hurt her if I told her about it.

My dad lives here in Portland. We have a pretty good understanding, although we aren't real close. He remarried six months after my mother died, and he was ostracized by all my mother's family because they thought it was a terrible thing for him to do.

Since I had a not-approved-by-society relationship, I could understand what he was going through. While it upset me that he did that, I told him everyone has their own grief to work out. He lost not only a lover, he lost his companion, and I realized that his loneliness and grief were different than mine. I still have a companion; I lost a mother. I told him I would want for him to be happy, whatever that meant. He really appreciated that, and I think it opened his eyes to other people's relationships.

Last summer, my brother was up here visiting from Colorado. He was over at my dad's house, out talking in the shop, and he said to my dad, "Well, what do you think of Rose and Jeri's relationship?" He knew Dad didn't know. Dad said, "What do you mean?" He said, "You know, that they love each other, that they're gay." Dad said very matter-of-factly, "I guess there's a little bit of that in all of us."

I've never talked to my dad about it. I've felt it isn't necessary until he's ready to talk about it. I don't hide anything from him. If he sees my name in the paper, or on television or something, that's fine. I don't think he's going to worry about it.

I only have that one brother. He's two years younger than I am, and he was around twenty-six when he found out five years ago.

When we lived in Grass Valley, we had a bunch of people from Metropolitan Community Church in San Francisco camping at our place one time. They pitched their tents in our backyard, and we just had a great time. My brother was living in the area, and he happened to come by the house when Rose and I were at church. Here were all these fairies running around the yard. One thing led to another, and one of the guys told him that they were all gay and that Rose and I were gay. I came home from church, and this guy came running out, wringing his hands and saying, "Oh, the worst has happened, the worst has happened. Your brother was here, and he knows we're all queer."

I really didn't know how to take that. I was relieved that I didn't have to be the one to tell him, but then I wondered how he reacted. He didn't come by for a day or two, and then we sat down and talked. He really couldn't believe it.

Through the years, he's accepted it quite well. He tells all his friends that his sister's gay and talks about my lover. Rose and I finally did get married in San Francisco in '71, and he brought his girlfriend to our wedding.

Maria Gonzales

I told my parents when I was twenty-one. I was working and living at home, and I couldn't deal with having somebody dictate my life.

I was fighting with my father, and he said, "You're living under my roof, you'll come in at midnight." I said, "Look, I have a different lifestyle." I went into my bedroom, and I told my mother, "I'm a lesbian." She just started crying. I didn't want to hurt her like that, but I couldn't take any more.

She said, "No, no, no, no, you can't say that," and she just held me. I said, "Mom, I am, and you have to realize that I am." She said, "When? When?" I said, "All my life, Mama, even since South Carolina." And then I told her about it. She said, "Why didn't you tell me? I could have helped you. You could have gone to a psychiatrist. Somebody could have helped you."

I said, "Mom, don't you understand? This is me. There is nothing wrong with me. I like being the way I am. Either you accept me for what I am or you don't, and if you don't, I'll leave." She said, "No, no, no, don't say that, don't say that. I love you, you're my daughter, I accept you, I accept you."

My mother told my father. He doesn't talk about it too much. I was on this TV program once with gay Latinos. Afterwards, he called me up and said, "I'm so proud of you. You were so good." I think he still flips out every once in a while. I don't expect them not to. It's hard for them to deal with.

They get embarrassed when my lover and I go over to their house, and they have company over, and I come out. He just goes, "Oh, no, here she is coming out again. She's always coming out to my straight friends. What am I going to do with her?"

My lover and I see my parents a lot. We stayed Christmas Eve over there and spent the night and slept together. One time, Mom says, "Somebody was talking about sixty-nine this and that." I said, "Well, Mom, that's how I do it." She said, "Yuk, don't tell me that." She totally flipped out, and I was cracking up.

My mom really loves my lover. Mom says she likes gay people better than she likes straights, because we're real. There's nothing phony about us. We're right out there.

My brother disowned me for a while. He said, "You're no sister of mine." I'd been trying to tell him all along. I don't think he really understood what I was saying until I was about eighteen or nineteen.

When I was twenty-one, I told him again before I told my parents. He said, "You're going to break Mom and Dad's hearts." I said, "I'm going to tell them." He wouldn't talk to me for a long time after that. But blood's thicker than water, as the saying goes.

I don't know how he takes it now. I think he's a little weirded out by it, because I think he's really a closet case himself. He really is. He's got a nice body. He's got an ass like a woman. He's had a shape all his life that's not really a little-boy shape but a little-girl shape. I ain't got an ass. My mother says, "There's some mix-up somewhere." I'm shaped like a football player, and he's shaped like a woman. I really think he's in the closet. We don't talk about me being gay. Not at all.

Chrystos

My family and I don't really get along, and we never have, so when I tell them, "I'm a queer," they say, "That's fine, dear, let's talk about the weather." They don't want to deal with it. They have no reaction at all. I have told them several times, and it just slides away.

They knew right when I first came out that I was lovers with a woman, and I've told them several times since, trying to get some kind of reaction out of them, but they aren't ever going to do that. They want to think that they're liberal and that it's fine that I'm a queer, but they give me ruffled blouses for Christmas.

My brothers pretty much accept me. I know my sister looks down on me, but she's never really come out and said anything. There's a lot of conflict between us, anyway. They were the first people in my family to know. I told them right when it was happening. They came to stay with my lover and me, and I told them what was going on.

Esther Brown

My parents just passed away—my mother this past April and my father the year before. I never told them. My one sister, who is currently partner in the ranch with me, knows. The only reason I told her was because my nephew came out here and spent the summers with me for four years. My nephew doesn't know. I told my sister, "I want you to know the situation, because if for any reason it comes up, I want you to be aware of it so we can work it out with Ralph. I don't want to embarrass you or Ralph because of the way I have decided to live. I didn't do it deliberately to hurt anyone. It's just my tendencies; I've admitted them, and that's just the way it is. You might think I'm cuckoo." And she said, "No, I don't."

I've always been a tomboy, always done what society considers the male work—like working on the cars and chopping

the wood and doing the chores that the boys should have
been doing but never did. If my dad needed a helper in
pouring cement or something, I was the one who had to help
because the boys were never around.

My nephew learned a great deal when he was here. When
he first started coming here, he was afraid to do anything.
His dad wouldn't even let him run the power lawnmower at
his house because he was afraid he'd hurt hisself. He'd never
been hunting or fishing or anything. So the four years he
was here, he learned to run all the equipment, to buck hay,
and to cut weeds with the chopper. After he was out here the
second year, he decided he wanted to work in the service
station because he wanted to be a mechanic like his auntie.
So he did, and he's still working in that service station. He's
becoming a great mechanic. But he would have died on the
vine if he hadn't come out here.

Rose

Unfortunately, when I lived at home my parents wouldn't
let me go out very often, because that's the way they were
brought up in Italy. Well, Jeri used to belong to a health spa,
so I joined it, also. That was very hard, because I went home
and my mother started screaming, "What did you do that
for? Don't you know no-good people go there?" Whoever
heard of no-good people? I didn't even know what a no-good
person was.

I started going there, and I started holding Jeri's hand, because the way I was brought up—which it is in Italy—women
are very affectionate with each other. When I came to the
States, I had a very difficult time walking by myself, because
in Italy I always held my girlfriend's hand, or we walked arm
in arm. Men do the same thing. Straight people do. So when I

met Jeri, I just automatically started holding her hand and that's how we started getting together, because then she started feeling for me, also, I guess. She fell in love, also. How romantic. That's how it all started, and we've been together ever since. It's been eleven years.

Jeri and I weren't in Oregon for very long. We ran away, because I couldn't move away from home. The way you were brought up when I lived in Italy, in the very old-fashioned small town that I came from, it doesn't matter whether you are a man or a woman, you don't leave home unless you are married. If you don't plan on getting married, then you just live with your parents and you have friends and relationships like that, but you just don't leave home. If you move away, then that means that you must be either whoring around or you must be a killer or a horrifying person. And so my parents had a little hard time to deal with it, but we ran away to Hawaii. My parents, they didn't know where we were, but I used to write to them at least once a month to let them know I was okay. I love my parents and we have a terrific relationship, but just that part, you know, was bad.

Then Jeri and I moved to San Francisco, and my parents came down to meet us for the first time. They came to our apartment. In two years I hadn't seen them. It was really quite a reunion. Ever since then, we've been the best of friends, and they just love Jeri as much as they love me. When Jeri became a Catholic and was baptized, they were her godparents.

I don't know if my parents know I'm gay. We never talk about it. They've never asked me, but we don't hide anything from them. The only thing we don't do is maybe kiss or hold hands. My parents travel with us if we go on a trip, and Jeri pays for everything for me, because that's how we always arranged it. It's not that we play any roles or anything, because we don't. Neither one of us believes in role-playing at all. Somehow, it's more comfortable if just one person handles the money, rather than both of us. If we go anywhere and my parents are around, she always pays for my stuff. We go to Reno together and I ask her for money to gamble with or she pays for my food, or if I go shopping with my mother and Jeri, I always ask Jeri if I see something that I like if I can have it. We don't hide anything. So it's pretty stupid if they don't know. They never asked. If they do, I'll tell them, "Yes," because I got nothing to hide. It's my life.

I have two brothers and a sister. One of my brothers I told. You see, Jeri's always part of the family; she's never excluded, never. He always used to tease me. He used to say, "Oh, when are you two going to marry each other?" Or he used to whisper in my ear, "I'm going to make her jealous." Well, I used to get a little uptight, but the only reason I did was because I knew Jeri was uptight. Otherwise, it didn't bother me a bit.

So one day I figured, since he knows already, anyway, I think I'll go tell him. Well, it was a rude awakening. I guess he didn't really know, because he said, "Oh, I was teasing you. I didn't mean for you to go and get married for real." I said, "Well, it's always been this way." He accepted it pretty good. He never said he had a hard time, or he never really expressed it, but I just felt the little tension there for a while. But now everything's comfortable.

My other brother never asked, but I'm sure he knows it, also. And my sister, I know she does, because she makes gay jokes all the time. So it's no big deal. We don't hide anything at all from my family. They know we own the house together, and they know we own the car together. So if they don't want to know, it's their business. It's their own head trip. Because I don't believe in hiding anything, especially from your family.

Canyon Sam

After I went away to college, I came back sometimes to visit my high school best friend. She had broken off with me to be with a man, and when I'd visit, we'd have these terrible scenes. After one scene, she called my parents over to her house, sat them down on the living room couch, and gave them a whole rap.

I was away at school, and I got this hysterical call from my mother. She said, "Pauline called us over and told us that you're neurotic and you're a lesbian and you're taking drugs and you're suicidal and you're alcoholic. Is this true?" I said, "No, it's not true, no, it's not true, no, it's not true. She's blowing the whole thing out of proportion. You know we're having hard times, but it's not that bad. I have a good life at school, and I'm into my work and my friends here." My parents accepted what I said.

Actually, my parents didn't use the word lesbian, and I don't know if Pauline used that word per se, but she got the idea across.

Later, at the time that I finally defined myself as a lesbian, I couldn't see telling my parents and being up-front about it. I knew I would buckle under, then, because they lay down very heavy trips. They would have really thrown stones. I wasn't worried about it, though, because I wasn't in that much involvement with them. I wasn't living close to them, and I was being very independent.

After I had related to women for almost two years, it got very uncomfortable with my parents because of the dishonesty. I would see them every few months for a week or so, and I just felt weird. They assumed I was the kid I always had been, when actually my values and my lifestyle were totally different and totally antagonistic to their own. I was frustrated and upset about it for weeks after my visits.

All the people I was around had been dykes for years, and they were out to their parents. Not necessarily with positive results or with positive relationships, but at least that was clean, and they didn't have to hide or repress who they were.

One afternoon I took a nap and woke up feeling real good; I must have had some nice dreams. I woke up thinking of the time when I had total support for who I was from intimate, personal friends, specifically two women who were role models for me. I got into that space totally and saw how much stronger and centered I felt in that space with the support of those people. Then I said, "Wow. I can tell them now. It would be real great to tell them right now."

I got the phone, came back to my bed, and got all covered with my blankets again, totally protected. Then I called my parents long-distance and told them. I said that the past few times I'd been with them, I'd felt uncomfortable because it was very dishonest, and that they should know my lifestyle and my values were totally different from theirs. One of the things was that I was into women, and that included sexually. I said I had made a real commitment to women.

My mother, of course, asked me, "Don't you think this is a phase?" She thinks everything I do is a phase. "Oh, you were into acting, and you were into dance for a while, and you were into taking pictures for a while. They're just phases." She can't stand when some person does more than one thing at once, especially when the things seem frivolous to her, like hobbies. She considers anything artistic a hobby. If I settled down to be a pharmacist or something, then she would consider that not a phase.

I said, "No. I never committed myself to any movement, to any community, to any theory, to any group before. I don't make commitments off the top of my head. This is the first one I've made, so I feel like it's real strong and will last for a while. I can't say it will be forever, because I would be a fool. I never speak like that. I don't know how I'll feel in five or ten years. I can say this feels very strong, and there is not a foreseeable future where this will be different."

Then I said, "If you're into knowing more about it, or knowing me, I'd be into sharing myself with you, but this is not open for debate or discussion. I'm not going to be open to you if you're going to judge me. If you're willing to accept who I am and you want to know more about me, I'd be willing to share myself with you." Total silence. Then I said, "I don't really expect you to respond to me right now; I just wanted to tell you this; so we can hang up because I'm finished."

I got a letter from them in a couple weeks, and they were basically calm. "You're our loving daughter, and we love you. Our home is always a haven to you. You just probably had a few bad experiences with some male friends." In other words, they really didn't accept it. They took it as a phase that I'm trying for a while, but they think I'll actually change back to normal.

Since then, it's gone downhill. Between that time and now, I've moved back down to the city where I am in contact with them a lot. When you're five hundred miles away and you communicate by letter every three weeks, it's different than when you have to be with them and they're laying trips on you all the time.

It's been six months since I came out to them, and they still have not accepted it. I'm not afraid they will disown me, because I can do without them more than they can do without me. They're always feeling afraid that I'm going to reject them and break off communication with them. I feel like they are real appreciative when I have contact with them, but they still try to convince me to change back.

Jane Salter

My parents live in Omaha, Nebraska. In December, a
couple of years ago, they came out here for a visit. I knew I
was going to have to tell them before they came, because
they would see gay women coming in and out of this house
all day long; a lot of people had keys to my house.

So I wrote them a long letter before Thanksgiving. I
talked about my life and about how glad I was that I had
gotten from them the courage to always stand by my convictions, to state who I was and what life meant to me. I said
I was a really strong person, and that had to come from
them. I certainly had many problems, but this was a more
satisfying way to live for me.

I told them I thought it was important for them to know,
because I felt I had been living a lie. Lesbianism was not a
matter of who I slept with, but a whole way of life for me.
I had built a family here, a supportive community where
we took care of each other. It was my lifeblood and very
important to me.

I was going with two women at the time, which made it
even harder to explain, in some ways. I think that parents
have an easier time accepting some kind of pseudohetero-
sexuality, some kind of monogamy or marriage, because they
at least understand the lifestyle. But they have no frame of
reference when you're not living that way. I wrote about
the two women I was seeing and tried to explain how they
were in my life—the things that we shared together and how
important those relationships were to me.

So I sent them this six-page typed letter, and I didn't hear
from them for a long time. I was freaked out of my mind.
One day the phone rang during the day, and it was my
mother. My mother never calls when the rates haven't gone

down. I thought, "This is it." It turned out she called then because my father wasn't home. I don't have much of a relationship with my father for all sorts of reasons, although I love him very much.

I said, "Why haven't you called me? I've been a nervous wreck." She said, "Well, we've had company for Thanksgiving and ya da da. I guess I knew, but I felt it never needed to be discussed." I said, "Well, that's typical. Nothing in our family ever needs to be discussed. I tried to tell you many times, but you cut me off most deliberately, and I didn't have the nerve to tell you." I had tried to tell her for years when I was young and confused, but she would say things like, "I remember reading *The Well of Loneliness*, and I've felt sorry for lesbians ever since." So I never had the nerve to say anything to her.

My mother wasn't upset. She has a great intellectual distance on life. The woman's so out of touch with any sort of feelings that it's unbelievable. She said, "You know, Jane, you left home early, you've always made your own decisions, you do what you want to do. You lead your own life, you do it well. You are an adult, you're the only one who can make decisions for yourself." She didn't say, "I'll respect those decisions," and even if she had, she would have been lying.

One of the women I was going with had a son, and my mother said, "Well, So-and-so has a son. That proves you're not born one way or the other." I think she wanted to relieve herself of whatever guilt feelings she might be having by saying I wasn't born this way.

While they were here, it was just hysterical. One day when my father wasn't with us, my mother started telling me what to do, which is very typical. "If I were you, I would stay with this lover. This one has so much more to offer you." It doesn't matter whether I'm queer or not, she's

going to run my life. "Marry this one." It made me furious,
but it was so like her.

My father didn't talk about it, but he reacted to one of
the women like she was the son-in-law. He would talk to
her about his real estate business and stuff. It was just
bizarre.

My lesbianism is accepted on some level by my family
because I'm blind. It's sort of like, "She went blind and
queer," except that my mother and I both know I've always
been queer.

I have two brothers. One is twenty-two, lives at home, and
sits in his room most of the time watching television. The
other one is a professor at Purdue, is married, and has a
daughter.

I told my sister-in-law before she was my sister-in-law that
I thought I was gay. Later, she started looking at other
women, which really upset me. I always wanted women to
find other women and be with other women because women
are so wonderful, but I didn't want her ever to leave my
brother. I never thought that I would have the creepy feelings I had. They're still together and very happy, which
makes me very happy.

I told my brother I was gay after the first time I slept
with a woman. It was the first time I had ever been turned
on in my whole life. I was just elated. So I called him on
the phone, because he is the closest member of my family.
He said, "Whatever makes you happy is good." But his
heart wasn't in it. I know that he wanted it to be, but it
wasn't. He had a lot of trouble understanding it, I think.

Later, he came here and met a lot of the women in my
life, particularly one woman that I was in love with, and
he was very attracted to her. After everyone left, we talked
about our attraction for the same woman, and it was a real
flip-out. It was his first real acknowledgment in a deep way

that that's where I was at. He had never seen me attracted to anyone in my life before, and he watched me being really into those women.

Now that my brother and my mother have spent a lot of time here, they both know how well all of us take care of each other and how much we all love each other.

Dolores Rodriguez

When I was in high school, my mother was constantly on my back: "Why don't you fix yourself up?" I would tell her, "Do you know why I'm wearing levis, and why I just have a T-shirt, and why my hair's messed up, and why I don't have makeup on, and why I hang around with a bunch of people and don't have a boyfriend? Because I'm a hippie." The hippie era and Haight-Ashbury gave me a cover. I kept clutching that cover because I was so afraid my father was going to figure out I was gay.

Finally, when I was in twelfth grade, I told my mother, "Look, I'm freaking out. Do you know why I'm freaking out? It's not because I'm on dope; it's not because I listen to acid rock; it's because I'm a lesbian. And if I get your understanding, then I'll be able to clean my life up. I can take this cover off."

She told me, "I always knew you were. If you're going to be a lesbian, be a good lesbian." And then she started crying. At first she was so glad that I wasn't freaking out because of her or dope, it was like, "Phew." Then it hit her, "Oh! A lesbian! That's just as bad. Aaaaaaaah!" She cried and cried.

When my mother left my father, people didn't think she was going to be able to raise her three kids. I think that's what hit her. "Maybe I didn't succeed. Maybe I didn't do it right."

The only thing I feel guilty about right now is that I am

my mother's only girl. You know how mothers are, especially
when you're the only girl. She always tells me she wants me
to have children. I tell her, "You've got to look at what's happening right now. Do you really want me to bring a child into
this world for life or just to satisfy you because you want
grandchildren?"

My family still thinks I'm going to grow out of being a
lesbian. They're still going along on, "One day you'll find the
right man. One day you'll realize that you have to live by
society's trip."

I just got back from home last night. She's never seen my
hair this short, and she didn't harp on it. She just kept saying, "So this is what it really is. You're not going to get married, huh?" I said, "Nope."

After I told my mother, she asked me, "Do you want me
to tell your brothers?" I said, "No, I don't want them to
know yet." But I think she couldn't handle it alone, so she
went to the supermacho of the family. He's eleven years
older than me, and he's a heavy drinker.

Here I am in bed one night, and he pulls me by one leg
and yanks me off the bed. He says, "So you want to be a man.
Okay, let's fight like two men." I was half asleep, and I said,
"Hey, man, get off it. Ain't nobody trying to be a man here.
I told Ma that I'm attracted to women and that I think I'm a
lesbian. I'd never interfere with your manhood. I'm not
trying to live up to what you are." But he still beat me up.
He punched me in the mouth, but my stepfather got in between us and threw my brother out of the house.

I didn't talk to him for about ten months, and we had been
really close. He finally came around and apologized. He said,
"You're weird, but you're my sister." He hasn't really accepted it; he's just put up with it.

My other brother is mellow. Whenever I had problems as
a kid, I would tell him, "Peter, let's take a ride to the country," and there we'd go. I went to him when I started my

period, because I didn't know nothing about periods. I said, "Peter! There's blood on my pants! What's wrong?" He sat down and explained periods and VD and pregnancy.

He asked me if I was a lesbian before I even told my mother. I said, "I think so. I've been feeling this way for a long time." He said, "Just keep your head together." He is a really far-out brother.

Carol Gay

When I lived in Mobile, my parents lived there, also. I took my gay friends over to their house for dinner, to watch TV, or to drop off my daughter Crystal so I could go to the bar. I told my folks I was going to the bar to go dancing, but I never said which bar. I never even thought that maybe they'd think something was funny.

Now that I think back about it, I wonder what my motives were in taking all these gay people over to the house. I guess I just figured my mother and father were dumb enough that they'd never realize, or if they did, it wouldn't matter to me, anyway.

My father's the type who doesn't give a shit what's going on, just so you're happy. We don't say much; it's not a real close family. My mother's the type who knows what's going on and sees it but doesn't want to acknowledge it. She won't ask me direct, because she knows I'd give her a direct answer back. If she asks, I'm going to say it. If she doesn't ask, I'll just let her go her happy way of not knowing, which is what she essentially wants.

I tell my mother what I'm doing. I say I'm living on women's land this summer, I'm going to this women's group and that women's activity. She knows I hang out only with women. It's not like I hide anything from her, but it's not like I'm going to offer it, either.

I have two brothers. One of them's a real conservative doctor and lives up North. I haven't seen him in years, and I
don't talk to him much. My other brother lives with my
parents. He's coming to visit here in a few months, so he'll
know when he gets here, for sure. I figure he'll just look
around and notice. I may not have to say anything. I don't
think I'd feel bad about telling him. I don't exactly know
how he'll accept it, but I think he'll be okay.

Vera Freeman

I didn't tell my parents for years. When I started going to
a psychiatrist, my mother kept asking me what was really
wrong with me, why was I going to a psychiatrist? I always
said, "I told you I'm going to a shrink to get my shit together,
can't you accept that?"

But one time, after a session with the shrink, I felt really
bad. The last thing I wanted was to get this letter from my
mother, wondering again what's wrong with me. So I just
grabbed a pencil and paper and said, "Well, Mother, you
asked for it. You want to know what's really wrong with me,
as you put it? I love women. I don't love men. Strange?
Well, that's the way I am."

I guess she passed my letter around to the whole family,
because my sister wanted to know, why did I tell her that? I
said, "Well, she wanted to know. I didn't tell her for years,
but she asked and I told her." I had promised the shrink
that if I was asked outright, I wouldn't deny who I am. To
anybody who counted, I would say, "Yes." I thought my
mother counted because she cares about me, and my father
cares about me.

My mother wrote back, and it was just an everyday letter
like before she had her answer. From all indications, it wasn't
upsetting my mother, but my sister was uptight about it. My

mother had a heart attack two months after that, and my sister came down on me and said I caused it, due to the letter. Of course, I thought I did. I told my shrink, and he said, "Two months later?" So he talked me out of that.

After I thought about it, I realized my sister and the ones who lived closer to my mom would be more likely to cause a heart attack than me. I've been away from the family since I was eighteen, going to school and raising kids, figuring ways to make myself a better person and giving glowing reports, not worrying my mother, not saying, "Hey, I'm strapped. Help." I took care of myself. I'm sure she appreciated that, because she was always talking to me how the other kids always needed help.

My father's never said anything. He probably knew all the time. Fathers somehow know.

I come from a large family of twelve children—seven girls, five boys. The ones who were home found out when my mother passed my letter around. Only that one sister came down on me then.

Two girls out of this family are very mentally disturbed. I tried not to make waves when I saw them the last time I was home. I was very careful to let them say whatever they wanted to and make no comment, because I finally learned that that's the way you handle it.

I have a gay brother. He moved away from home, too. He turned into an alcoholic. I'm not sure he knows I am gay. I don't see him. When my mother passed the letter around, he wasn't home, and then when I went back for my mother's funeral, he didn't show up. As a matter of fact, I haven't seen him since the last riot they had in Milwaukee.

Mary Howland

I did not tell my parents when I first came out. However, when they came to visit me in December of 1972, I intended to share this with them. I thought, "If they're going to spend eight days with me, I'm not going to ask all my friends to stay away and hide all my literature. I'm going to come out to them. My being gay is not some affliction. It's a very joyful part of me."

The day they arrived, I fell and sprained my leg. I met my folks at the door on crutches, knowing that for a month I was going to have to be down with my leg up. I also knew my parents well enough to know that I was not going to come out to them when I was flat on my back, because I wouldn't be able to get away from them. I couldn't make space for myself or take care of myself. So I did not come out to them then.

They met many of my friends, read my feminist literature, and we had a lot of good talks. At the end of that eight days, they asked me if a couple of my friends were lesbians, and I said, "Yes, they are." They made several comments like, "What a tragic thing to do to your parents," so I figured they weren't quite ready yet. When they left, they said, "We're very confused. None of our five children are living the way we taught them to live, but we love them all very much." For them, that acceptance was a tremendous thing, because it meant that they had to rethink their very foundations.

Finally, last June, after Lisa and I had been together well over a year, I thought, "Okay, I'm going to come out to them. I don't have anything to lose, and I have a lot to gain—that is, a very real relationship with them."

I sat down at the end of my two-week vacation and wrote a ten- or twelve-page letter. "Dear Mom and Dad, Lisa and I have been really busy with our house." I wrote all about the stuff we'd done with *our* house and *our* dog and the landscaping we'd done on *our* yard. Then I talked about Lisa graduating from college and about the three-day workshop we led at a conference on lesbians for lesbians. I talked about the contents of the workshop, which we, of course, had to conjure up ourselves, and talked about going out with the other women to celebrate Lisa's birthday.

In other words, I reported on my two-week vacation in a very warm, natural style. I was so tired of writing, saying, "The dogs are fine and the cats are fine and I'm fine and Lisa's working and I love my job." So I wrote the kind of letter I'd always wanted to write, but I didn't ever say, "I'm a lesbian." I just assumed they already knew.

A month went by from the time I wrote that letter until the time I got a response, and the response was a ninety-minute tape from them. I thought, "Oh, boy, here we go." Well, eighty minutes of it was my dad's blow-by-blow account of their trip to Canada. His only comment about my letter was, "It was really great to hear from you. I hope you write long letters again."

My mom did the last ten minutes. She said that she enjoyed our letter and that she thought we were both working too hard and keeping much too busy for our own good. She said, "You two take care and write again." That's all.

I knew they got the message, though, because on my birthday in April, my brother Dave and his wife called me from Tampa. Dave said, "I hear you told the folks you were gay." I said, "Yeah. How did you know?" He said, "Well, Dad wrote us a twelve-page letter all about his trip to Canada, and he said, "Mary told us in her last letter she was a lesbian. Mom's been trying to tell me that for two years and I wouldn't believe her, but now I have to believe her because Mary said it herself." Dad hadn't asked for an opinion, he hadn't offered a judgment, he hadn't said he was crushed or happy or anything. He had just made that statement.

Since that time, the letters continue to come and go. There's no more mention of the subject, except that I did put my folks on the mailing list of the Metropolitan Community Church, because I felt that reading about homosexuality in Christian terms was something they could relate to.

When I talked to my mom a couple of weeks ago on the phone, she said, "Did you send me those brochures?" I said, "What brochures?" I knew which ones they were, but I made her tell me. I said that I had had them sent to her, and I said, "Do you mind?" She almost choked on her words, and she said, "Oh, no. I'm interested in anything you're interested in."

Shortly after I came out, I came out to my brother Dave, because he and I are so close. He and his wife, who is a nurse, now live in Florida, and they've been really supportive.

Then my brother Dan, who has a high position in the federal government, figured it out and wrote me a letter about a year and a half ago. He is steeped in great religious principles, and we've had almost a stereotypical dialogue in letters about what's sinful and what isn't, what's natural and what isn't, what's God's will and what isn't.

My eldest brother and my youngest brother probably know, but they haven't ever said anything to me.

Olivia Moreno

When I was young, I would talk to my mom about what girls I liked. She said, "Well, if you feel that way, there's nothing I can do about it, but maybe you shouldn't talk about it in public." I'm sure she thought it was a phase. All little girls, whether they're straight or gay, have crushes on older teachers and other women.

Sometimes when she'd get mad, she'd bring it up. She'd say, "Just because you want to be a man doesn't mean you can get away with bossing me around." I'd say, "Mother, I don't want to be a man. I really don't."

My mom met my first lover when Patty and I were saying

good-bye. We'd lived in the dorms together for eight weeks. I didn't tell her about Patty and me, but when I got in the car, my mom said, "You really love her, don't you?" I said, "Yeah." She said, "I can tell."

My lover's mother wasn't as understanding. In fact, she kicked me out of their house. We were in Patty's bedroom. I was laying on the bed, and Patty had her arm on my leg. We were just talking, and her mom walked in and said, "There's something not normal about this relationship. I think you should leave." So I left. I didn't want to cause hassles, because Patty was only sixteen and had to live at home for a couple more years. I didn't want to cause a lot of flak between her and her parents. So we broke up.

I told my mom for sure that I was gay about four months ago. I said, "Mother, you know that I'm gay?" I gave her one of the Gay Youth cards that I carry around in my wallet and said, "Look what I'm into, Mom." She said, "Well, if that's your trip, that's okay."

My mom told me a long time ago that the only thing she would ever really be down on me for was if I had an abortion. She's probably relieved that I won't ever do that. When I do get pregnant, it will be because I intentionally set out to get pregnant. She probably sees advantages and disadvantages to my being gay.

She's really mellow about it. I can take my lovers home with me for Christmas and sleep with them, and stuff. They're just as welcome as my sisters-in-law.

I have eight brothers—three older and five younger. Three live back in Cincinnati with my father, so I don't have to deal with them. They're young, anyway—like seven, five, and four.

My three older brothers are fairly conservative. They don't know much about my being gay, because they were out of the home when I started going through this transition. I don't know if they know for sure or not.

My other two brothers are seventeen and sixteen. They both know. They really don't know how to deal with it. I never went to them and said, "I'm gay," but they probably just picked it up, because it's very open in my house.

My brother used to like this friend of mine that I liked, too. When he said he liked her, I said, "Good choice." I was kind of patting him on the back and saying, "Right on. Do it to it." He wasn't surprised; he just accepted it. They usually tease me about it.

If my brothers lived here in Olympia, I probably wouldn't be as open as I am now. They have to go to high school, and I wouldn't want them to be teased or to have to put up with the shit that might happen.

I still haven't come out to my grandfather. He lives in Cathlamet, Washington. When I go down there, it's only for a couple of days, and we usually end up arguing. We had a theoretical conversation about gay people last time I was there. He asked me if I didn't think that two women living together and having sex together was the most disgusting, repulsive thing in the whole world. I said, "No, I really don't think so." He got up and left, and I got up and left, and that's the last time we talked about it.

Mrs. Hite

HOW DID YOU LEARN THAT YOUR DAUGHTER IS A LESBIAN?

Olivia didn't tell me in so many words. She hinted around at first, until I had the idea before she told me outright. She had always said she really didn't like guys that well. It seemed to me that she went out with them mainly because the other girls did. She had a pretty bad stepfather, I think, which turned her off men.

After she went to college, she finally sat down and decided to tell me. I don't remember exactly what she said—I've got so many children. She said she hoped that I wouldn't be mad about it and thought that I could probably understand. It kind of came as a shock, really, but I have the opinion that people have the right to love who they please.

I felt a little strange, thinking, "Now, what will people think if they know I've got a daughter that's along that line?" But then I thought, "Well, what the heck. Why do other people matter? They're my kids, and I like them however they are. It's a part of her, so I'll take her like she is."

She's my daughter. If she had a broken leg, I wouldn't say, "Hey, go away. I don't want you anymore." Or if she had a mental disease, I wouldn't say, "Hey, get out of here." This is the way I feel she was born or developed, and she couldn't help being the way she is. Why deny a person a chance to have somebody they love just because they don't happen to be the same as a lot of people? I've never been particularly conventional. I've never really done just what people think I should all the time.

Once in a while, I wonder if she's lesbian all the way, because I know she has liked boys. I wonder whether she'll stay that way and how her life will be later on if she continues that way. But she's a grown person. She's going to have to worry about her own life and how she runs her life. I don't suppose I run my life to suit her.

I'm a homebody. I really don't have a whole lot of close friends, so it doesn't come up in conversation. You don't walk up to somebody you know at square dancing and say, "Hey, have I told you my daughter's a lesbian?" That would be a little weird to do. They'd look at you like, "What's the matter with you, lady?" If anybody asked, I don't think I'd be afraid to admit it.

I'm not really close enough to anybody but my own family to talk about it. With them, I feel that if Olivia wants them to know, she should tell them. I don't know if all of her brothers know it. If I get a chance and something comes up on TV about lesbianism or homosexuals, I try to get in that people are not always the same but they have the right to have the life that they feel is right for them.

Tonya Holloway

It took me a long time to decide, "Do I tell my mother or don't I? If I tell my mother, does she take my kid away? How much of my life does my mother need to know in order for us to have a relationship?"

Before this, my mom and I had had a very good relationship, and our relationship was getting hurt because I wasn't talking to her as much. I had been going over to her house every other night, just to talk. But then I started not talking to her for two weeks at a time, and she would call me up and say, "I haven't heard from you. Anything wrong?" "No, I've just been busy." "Well, okay. Why don't you bring Daniel by? We'd like to see the grandkid."

When my father moved down to San Francisco and my mother moved in with me, that was really hard. I couldn't be myself in my own house. I felt like I had to hide all my magazines, and I felt like I had to hide myself. It got to the point where I didn't like her being there. I had to tell her or we just would have broke off, and she's really one of the best friends I have.

For weeks I tried to find some way to slip in a "Well, so am I" type thing. I'd say things like, "It would be better if all women were lesbians," and she'd go, "Oh, yeah, probably." And that would be it. The conversation had to be just right, and I couldn't get it to that point.

She went up to Bear Lake for a week and a half, and she took Daniel. When she came back, she naturally wanted to know what I did with all my free time. I said, "Well, I went to a birthday party." She said, "Did Liz go with you?" I said,

"No, because we're all lesbians, and she's not." She just said, "Oh," and then started talking again about I don't know what. I didn't hear her after that point.

We were sitting at this gas station, and I was gripping the steering wheel, thinking, "React, Mother. Say something. Do something. Scream. Hit me. Yell. Jump up and down, I don't care." Nothing. And that was the last time we talked about it for months. I just figured, "Tomorrow I'm going to get out of school and Daniel will be gone, and my mother will be gone and she'll take him away from me." It was really heavy. I was too scared to say, "Well, what do you think of that?" It was hard enough just to say that much.

About two months later, we invited the mothers to the lesbian support group. I said, "You know that support group that I've been going to? Well, it's a lesbian support group." She goes, "Yeah." No reaction. I said, "Well, we'd like the mothers to come and I'm inviting you, and I hope you'll come." She said, "I just don't understand." I said, "You don't have to understand me; you just have to accept me." So she came to the support group, and she still doesn't understand me, but that's all right.

I don't think it was that much of a shock to her. Ever since I realized the difference between men and women and saw what they did to each other, I told her how weird I thought men were. When I was fourteen years old, I told her, "You know, if I want a kid, I'm not going to get married." I was sixteen years old, and I said, "I will never marry. I think it's a bore. Men are really stupid." I've been telling her these things since I was a little kid.

They used to call me the women's libber of the family. At one time my brother was the last Holloway, and if he didn't get married and have a son, there wouldn't be any Holloways left. So I told my grandmother, with my mother and everybody sitting there, "Well, Grandma, I'll get pregnant and have a boy to carry on the Holloway name for you." This was when I was in the tenth or eleventh grade.

My mother's always been the one to tell me, "Go get a good job; don't depend on some man to support you. Make sure you can do it yourself." So she's known how I feel for a long time.

The second time I talked to her, she did say, "What about Daniel?" I said, "Well, the few men in his life are good men and not weirdos. I'd sooner have a few good men than a whole bunch of weird men in his life." She said, "I don't understand you."

I think she's not too worried about it now. My life isn't that different from what it has been for the last couple of years, except for the lack of men. That's the only difference in my life, and I think that's a good difference.

So my relationship with my mother is back to the way it used to be. We still have heavy conversations; we just don't have them about lesbians. But then I don't feel a need to explain to her why I'm the way I am. She's gone through all my ups and downs and freak-outs with me, so I'm sure she's bound to know why I am the way I am. And if she can't understand it, or if she thinks she's got to understand it, well, then, she can ask me.

―――――――――――

I'm twenty-five. I was born in Concord, California. I'm the middle of three kids. My mother and father have been married their whole life; they're very conservative-type people, in a way. My father always believed that the man was the ruler of the house, and my mother went along with him because she was married to him. Now I live in a house by myself with my son and my dog and five cats. I was on welfare for four years. I'm off it now, working as an RN.

Mrs. Holloway

HOW DID YOU LEARN THAT YOUR DAUGHTER IS A LESBIAN?

She didn't come right out and say it. She'd mentioned little things, and then a few months ago—before she moved into her own house—she mentioned that there ought to be more gay people like us, or something. So when she just made this statement, I knew that she was and wondered why, how, and all of that.

I don't know how long she has considered herself a gay person. When she lived in Sonoma, she used to go to the gay bars, but she also dated men. This was before she went to Hawaii and before she had the baby. Since she came back from Hawaii, she hasn't dated anymore and hates men, I presume. I mean, the way she acts, she does. So I never had any question before about her being gay until that statement was made.

When she made this statement, I didn't think too much about it. I guess you try to put these things out of your mind.

Of course, I've always been one that likes the secure feeling of having the husband to take care of me. I wondered, "How do they take care of themselves? How would she take care of her child?" If I were sick, my husband would take care of me; if she's sick, there's no one.

I did say to Tonya, "I don't understand," and she said, "Well, you don't have to." I really don't know why people are gay people. I can love you; I can love all other people. But to really love, I would have to love a man. I don't understand how women can actually feel and make love, because to me there is the sexual part of love that is love. I don't understand how women can have this type of love, but it doesn't bother me. Of course, Tonya has never had a lover living with her. Maybe if that were to happen, it might bother me; I don't know.

Now, maybe if Tonya had come in and said to me, "This is Ruth, and Ruth is gay" I may have thought, "Gee, what's wrong with that kid?" or, "Why is she this way? I don't know if I want my daughter associating with her."

Many people think that there is something wrong with people that are gay, and this is just a normal thought. I did get the impression from the young ladies at the gay support group meeting, and I get it from my Tonya, also, that they must have been awfully hurt by men to turn their affections and their love only toward women. I felt a lot of them were so extremely hurt by fathers, stepfathers, brothers, and other men that maybe they cannot trust another man, and they can feel close and comfortable with a woman instead. This is my own version of it. I just don't know why people become gay. As I say, to me it's just as easy to love a man as it is to love a woman. And so unless they have been hurt a lot by men, well, then, why do they turn to women for love?

I do know that Tonya has been hurt. I think she feels that men use women, period. She has said to me, "I could never live with my own father as a husband. How can you live with him?" She's a very strong person now. She never really used to be, but she is now, and she's not going to give in to anyone. She's not going to be waiting on any man or darning any man's socks.

I've never said anything to anyone other than my younger daughter and a sister-in-law who is very close to me. Other than that, I don't talk about it. If something were said to me like, "Gee, do you every worry about Tonya being gay?" I would probably say, "No, I don't worry, because she is." You don't go on hiding it. I have some friends and they say, "Gee, is Tonya ever going to get married?" I say, "No, she hates men," and that's where it ends. And it's true. Maybe not all men, no. She has some friends that are men, but she hates men to the point where she would not marry one.

I've always felt, live and let live. If they're happy and

they're not hurting anyone, then why be all upset about them? You may not like the way I live, but would you try to hurt me, or would you try to make me feel that it is a wrong way to live? People have been gay for hundreds and hundreds of years. I believe in the Ten Commandments, and I don't believe there's anything in the Ten Commandments that says you cannot be a lesbian, or you cannot be a heterosexual. I say, to each his own. I wish that other people could be more tolerant.

The only thing that bothers me is that I'd like to have a jillion grandchildren, and I won't have a jillion grandchildren. I have one, and I'm very fortunate to have him, although I worry about him in this respect: he is so attached to Tonya and me. He loves Papa, my husband, but Papa's the only man he's got. He doesn't have any uncles or any brothers. Sometimes this can be hard on the child, because the mother can be very domineering, whether she knows it or not. She needs a father or another man to step in once in a while to say, "Hey, that's wrong. You're telling him the wrong thing. Let's sit down and discuss this; I want to explain a man's view."

Papa is there to fix his toys, and Papa is there to play a game with him, but Papa's not there enough. He needs, right now, to be able to go with some boys and learn how to play ball. His mama can help, but I still think he needs this from boys. Is she going to be able to teach him fishing and hunting and the things that she doesn't like?

A woman can be very firm, and she can spank and she can correct, as mothers all do, but there's nothing like a man to say, "No. Just no." It's funny how they always listen more to the man. God made woman and man, so you have to learn to live with both women and men. He should be taught a few things by the man and not be with just women all the time. I don't think that's healthy. I really don't.

Jesse Linn

At the time I came out to myself, I thought, "Well, I'll never tell my mother, but if she finds out, I'll try and talk to her." I've always been close to her and so I wanted to share that with her, but I was afraid she would get more pain out of it than I would get enjoyment. So I protected her from it for a while.

Then she started asking me if I was gay in roundabout ways. One time she asked why I had all these gay albums in my house. Another time I was looking at a picture of her and another woman, and I asked her who that woman was. She said, "Oh, that's when I was in my lesbian relationship." I nearly fell out of my chair.

She told me that years ago when she was a teacher, she had shared a house with another woman who was also a schoolteacher. The superintendent of the school thought they were lesbians, which wasn't true, so he didn't rehire them the next year. I was pretty aware at that time that she was trying to get some response from me.

One night a male friend was going to be spending the night at my house. My mother was also spending the night and was sleeping on the couch in the living room. Doug was going to be in later, so I told my mother, "If you hear somebody coming in later, it's just Doug, so don't worry about it."

She said, "Oh, is he coming to see you?" My first thought was, "Oh, here it comes again." I almost said to her, "Mother, I don't sleep with men." I was halfway angry at her for probing me and halfway wanting just to tell her, but still being afraid that it would give her pain.

She said, "I guess I shouldn't pry into your personal life." But then she went on about how it doesn't ever seem to her that I have relationships with any of the men who come around here. I said, "Well, I don't," and I told her I'd talk to her about it the next day. It was really late. That night I went to bed feeling real jittery. I knew the time had come, and that I couldn't wriggle out of it this time.

The next morning I told her I was gay, that I felt really good about it, and that I was afraid of hurting her. She said, "Well, I guess I've been wanting to know that. I've been suspecting it for a long time, but I just wanted you to be the one to tell me." She was being real supportive of me, and I said, "You've been suspecting it for a long time?" She said she'd been suspecting it for about four years, which was two years before I was even aware of it!

As I told her my feelings, it was really important to me that she didn't think I was relating to women now because I had bad experiences with men, or that I was loving women as a second choice. It was also important to me that she know I was really happy, that I didn't feel bad about myself, or perverted or immoral. I wanted her to know how good and whole I felt.

She was very supportive. She told me she didn't completely understand, but she wants to understand. She wanted me to tell her about my feelings and some of my experiences so she could get rid of her stereotyped images.

So, my mother knowing has turned out to be a very positive experience. I probably could have told her earlier, but I just didn't realize she was going to be that open. I mean, she's sixty-five years old.

––––––––––

I'm a student, twenty-six years old. I was raised in Vallejo, California. My parents gave me a lot of independence, because they were older and they didn't know if they'd always be there. In the tenth grade, I became a hippie, and I stayed a hippie until I was twenty-three. I was already aware of class oppression, and I didn't want to become an oppressor. I knew what it was like to be oppressed because I was raised in a working class family, so my answer to that was to sort of drop out and live a simple, free lifestyle. I got married for a month. I got pregnant, and as soon as I found out I was pregnant, I didn't want to be married anymore.

I just love going to school. This is all hypothetical, but right now I feel like I'll go into Women's Studies.

Mrs. Linn

HOW DID YOU LEARN THAT YOUR DAUGHTER IS A LESBIAN?

About a month ago, I was staying overnight at Jesse's, and I was sleeping down on the davenport. She was getting ready for a test the next day and didn't want to be disturbed in her sleep. My dog does disturb her on the foot of the bed, so I slept on the davenport. She had studied late into the evening —until midnight, at least—and she had to get up at 6 A.M. the next morning. She had turned out most of the lights and was getting ready to go upstairs.

There was a young gentleman who was coming in later to stay for the night, but all the beds seemed to be full around the house. Just in a kidding manner I said, "Where in the world is he going to sleep? I've got the davenport." I kind of grinned at her and said, "Your room?"

She said, "No." Then she stood there for a long time deep in thought and didn't say anything. I said, "After all, with the communal living, I assumed there were sleeping arrangements like that." She said, "No. Well, I'll tell you how it is."

We talked maybe five minutes or so, but we didn't go into it much. I told her that I had had a suspicion because of the pictures and some of the literature that was around the place. She said she had been wanting to tell me for a long time, because it made her uneasy that she was keeping something from me. We have a close relationship. Then she said she was tired and wanted to get to bed.

The next morning, she gave me a report she had written on homosexuals and asked me if I would like to read it. I think she knew I wasn't going to chastise her. When my girls became adults, I let go of them completely. I didn't try to live their lives, even though there were things that I wouldn't have had them do. If they made mistakes, it was their responsibility.

As a parent, you have a succession of problems that throw you, and you just have to roll with each wave as it comes in. A lot of parents do go under and think, "Oh, dear, where did I go wrong?" Well, if you feel you always did the best you could, if you did go wrong, it wasn't willingly; it was maybe because you didn't know. But I wouldn't say that her father and I went wrong anywhere, as far as Jesse was concerned.

In my family and in Jesse's father's family, women were very highly respected. They were on equal terms with the men. They were the queen on the throne and the power behind the throne, in all respects. Jesse can't say she ever saw women subdued in her own family. So I don't know, maybe her own two marriages had an influence on her choice.

I can't say that I approved when she told me. I still don't, but like I say, it's her life. I think my reaction was one of relief that she had told me and settled my mind, more than anything else. I appreciate the fact that Jesse is close friends with me. I think it's a much closer relationship than the continual mother-daughter relationship where one is dominant and the other is submissive.

Kathy O'Keefe

I knew from the beginning that I couldn't tell my dad. He and I were just beginning to relate to each other on a very basic human level, after several years of not being able to relate at all because of his problems. He's always been so absent in the brain and the emotional part of him, not knowing where I am physically in the world or what I'm doing at a given point in time. He'd say, "Do you have a job?" when I'd have been in school for seven years. He's just not quite aware of what's going on. So I didn't want to tell him, and he's physically removed enough from my hometown that I didn't worry about it.

I told my mother as soon as possible, about a month after I told my sister Shelly, and two months after I came out. We have the kind of relationship where I couldn't *not* tell her. If I didn't tell her, that would mean that I couldn't go home, and I go home all the time. Or I would have had to have left Mona, my lover, here. I didn't ever think of not telling her.

I assumed she would accept it, that she would really understand and be happy that I was finding happiness for myself. I wrote her this letter on the twenty-first of April:

Mama,
    If you are confused at this point, I guess I can tell you what you may have, in your center, already begun to realize. I'm in the process of opening up, and that process has shown me new ways of relating to people of all sizes, ages, and sexes. Mona is a woman my age who sees in me certain qualities she wants to experience. And I find her wit and her strength fascinating and fresh. We are each of us trying to find love and fulfillment and have turned to each other.
    So I have a woman lover, and while this experience alone does not make me a lesbian, or gay, or whatever label, I find more and more that, for me, women are supporting and allowing me to evolve into the creative artist and person that I will be. And that men I have

known and continue to meet don't give me the space I
require to be a whole person. I have good relationships
with gay and straight people alike, and I'm not retreat-
ing from meeting life's challenges, but I'm fully aware
of the challenge I face as a lesbian artist in this weird
and conservative world.

I think lesbian is a beautiful word, and even though
your experience with women as supporters and nurtur-
ers has been and is not wholly conjunctive with my experience, I think that the roots of that disharmony are
deep and very old and that freeing yourself of the dis-
trust of the past, by opening yourself up to the women
of the present, could afford you much happiness. Shelly,
too.

I'm as happy now as I have been at my happiest time,
even though the flow is broken momentarily as small
bits of old experiences are brought back to me in tests.
I am headed for an unfolding of energy power I have
never known before.

I love you all, and I know my happiness is the sign by
which you read my life. The days and weeks are foreign
to you by the distance yet between us. The future cannot be dealt with honestly until the past is resolved.
And my turning over of stones has shown me many
things, beautiful and ugly. I am in the present a lot for
the first time since I was a small child, and it's a good
feeling to know that my life is my own now and not
belonging to a former self, a faker and self-delusive
child, nor belonging to a future I can't fully define.

So I shot that off in the mail. I don't really remember her
reaction. I remember her being very supportive and writing
something like, "Whatever makes you happy will make me
happy." But then again, I think her initial reaction was a
mixture of jealousy and hurt. Because we are such a close

family—there are just my mom, my sister, and I—anyone who comes into that sphere of three usually really has to deal with the other two. The men my mother related to after my parents divorced were very heavily scrutinized by my sister and me. My mother's reaction to my letter was mild compared to what one guy got from us.

The only negative reaction I got from her was because Mom and Shelly and Shelly's husband and I planned to go to Mexico for Easter vacation. It was going to be a family trip, just the four of us. I assumed that Mona and I would come down and go, too. My mother's reply to my sister—and my sister related it to me, which is how the communication usually goes; we're go-betweens for each other—was that Mom had thought it was going to be just the four of us, and here I was bringing a complete stranger along. She reacted quite normally, since she had expectations about what we were going to be doing. She never came out front to either Shelly or me and said, "I don't want Mona to come along." She just stopped communicating about it.

Then the next thing I knew, she called me up on the phone and said she'd bought this new sofa bed for the living room, so Mona and I would have a place to sleep when we came down at Easter to go to Mexico. I was astonished.

So we all went to Mexico and had one of the best times of our lives. We slept in the same motel room, slept in the same tent. Mom seemed a little nervous at first, but then she found out Mona could play cribbage and Scrabble, so that was it. They were fast friends immediately. We played cards and went swimming on the beach and clowned around and got drunk. That's all it took.

Mona and I met in March. In April, I brought my sister Shelly up here with me because it was close to her twenty-first birthday, and I wanted her to see where I was living. I had already written her a couple of letters; she knew I was a lesbian, and it was fine with her. In fact, the day we got up here, I called Mona and she came over, and we all slept together in the same bed in Mona's room because my sister didn't want to sleep out on the couch.

When Shelly was here, it was the first time she'd been away from home in a long time. It was the first time she'd ever been separated from her husband, and here she was in this house full of women. I was with Mona; another couple, Julie and Becky, were there; the Women's Studies festival was happening at Sonoma State; and I was selling rummage and costumes for the Women's Center, dragging my sister along with me.

Every day she was at our house, she wrote, and when she left, she left her writing. I called her up and said, "You left all this stuff." She said, "Oh. I guess I left it there for you to read."

One of the things she wrote was, "Julie and Becky's relationship has dispelled my few questions about gay relationships. Love is love. Anyway, I really feel close to Julie, or rather that I could be her friend, because she has a touch of the craziness—that certain quality I really identify with." Then she wrote about Mona. "Mona is a warm, friendly woman. I don't usually bother to take the time to study women, but she is close to my sister, so I actually studied her. Kathy tells me of her intelligence, but to me having smarts doesn't matter. I just know I really like her. I also wish Kathy could loosen up." And, "I may not know much, but I thought the reason two people of the same sex could be closer lovers was because they felt less pressure, were more in tune with each other's fantasies and lives." She was saying that because of the way I was acting at the time. I was being kind of apprehensive, not about Shelly being there, but just relating to Mona. I was still unsure about it, especially since this was right after Mona had been seeing another woman. I didn't really know what was happening, but I was still plugging my energy into the relationship.

Anyway, so my sister just walked right into the situation, and that was that.

———————

I'm twenty-five. I was born in southern Oregon in early May of 1951. That makes me a Taurus with a Pisces rising, and my moon is in Taurus. I'm very organized. The women in my family on both sides are real close to each other. I have a bachelor's degree in psychology and a bachelor's degree in theater arts. I'm also a certified preschool teacher. I taught preschool for a while, and since 1974, I've been teaching dance and choreographing. I'm working now with a collective of five women in dance theater.

Mrs. O'Keefe

I think Shelly told me about Kathy, and then Kathy wrote to me later. I didn't know what to think or what to say. It was somewhat of a shock. Although I have gay male friends, you just don't think that about your own children. So it took me probably two or three months before I could sort it all out in my mind.

I think at the very beginning I was disappointed. I don't know why. I guess because it was my child. I felt, "Too bad," or whatever. I couldn't tell anyone, or I didn't tell anyone for quite a while, because you don't open a conversation with, "Oh, by the way . . ." I have no other friends who have gay children, or if they do, they would never in the world admit it.

I had a sense of depression for a while. I don't think it was because I knew she was gay; I think most of it was because I didn't know what to say to her. I wanted to say something, but I wanted it to be the right thing. I don't see Kathy that often, and it's hard to put all your feelings in a letter.

It was in my mind constantly, and I'm a very busy, active person. But when I get something like that on my mind, I have to think it out. If I could have seen her, it might have been a different thing. The fact is, I don't see her that often, and it was during a time when I couldn't go up there, and she couldn't come down here. Of course, it's easy to write things and tear them up and rewrite them, but I don't usually do that. I write like I talk, and once I get it down on paper—whether it's right or wrong—that's what they get.

Then all of a sudden, it became very easy. She was happy, and this was what she chose. If she had chosen to marry a Black person, or whatever, that's her choice. I've never really tried to regulate my children's lives.

I know I wasn't shocked to the point of thinking, "Oh, how could it happen to me?" because a lot of things have happened to me. Neither one of my kids is perfect, and I've gone through everything they've gone through. They've never had to go around the corner and hide things from me. It pleases me immensely they feel enough confidence in my love that they can tell me. I know a lot of parents who know nothing about what their kids do.

Kathy's a very sweet person. I know in the back of my mind I kept waiting for some signs of masculinity to show up in her. I guess that's a common thing that you look for. But it hasn't changed her for anything but the better.

Even the first time I met Mona, I never did have any animosity. I like Mona. We all went to Mexico together, and it was just the most natural thing in the world. Brad and Shelly were together, and Kathy and Mona were together. We were a family, off on a family vacation.

Kathy and Mona came down and stayed in the living room where the sofa makes into a bed. I'd get up in the morning when they'd be in bed together and I kept thinking, "Gee, why don't I feel funny, or something?" But it just never occurred to me.

I never have referred to Mona as her lover. In fact, when I told one gay friend of mine about Kathy and Mona, he said, "Well, I sure hope you don't call her Kathy's lover." Male homosexuals don't like that term. I just call her a friend.

I had been around gay people before. I used to work in New York, and like in San Francisco, there are colonies. But most of them were male–female impersonators in night-clubs. I thought they were hilarious.

I've been in San Francisco a lot of times, and I've watched these men walk down the street—they're trying so hard to be feminine and swish their hips good. I love to watch them. I think they're funny.

My ex-husband and I went up to San Francisco about ten years ago. We were drinking and out on a lark. We'd seen a fantastic show at a gay men's club, and we said, "Well, let's go see what the other half looks like. We drove up and down the street where there are all kinds of clubs, but we couldn't find any lesbian clubs. They had places, but nobody knew, not even the cabdrivers, and cabdrivers know everything. I guess since we'd seen all these men dressed up like women —dancing in a chorus line—my thoughts probably were that if we went to a lesbian bar, they'd all be dressed up like men.

The first real close gay friend I had was a young man who played beautiful piano in a hotel here in town. I don't know how, but I knew he was gay when I first met him. He and his lover and I were very good friends. We went to the beach all the time and drank champagne. We'd go to the city for dinner, just the three of us. I know there were people in town, bigoted people, who probably thought it was very strange for two gay men and me to be running around and obviously having a very good time. I never cared what other people thought about it, because my life's my life. Whatever I do, I do. I lived with a man for six years, and Shelly lived with us, too. It was very natural. He was a lot younger than I was, and there was no reason to get married. We were a family. So that's the way I feel with Kathy and Mona. They're my family.

I would like my ex-husband to know about Kathy, because after all, she's his child, too. But that's up to Kathy. I wouldn't call him up and say, "Guess what?" It's going to be very hard for Kathy to break this to him. He'll probably want her to go to a shrink. He'd say she's not all right upstairs, you know. I'm sure it would embarrass him to have other people know, but most of the people I have contact with don't see him anyway. Probably nine-tenths of the people we knew as a couple years ago would say, "Gee, I'm sorry about Kathy. It's terrible."

I don't even think about it in my everyday routine. I know that at one time I thought of very little else, but I never think about it now. I think of Kathy and Mona, but I don't think of them as two females. It just seems such a normal thing to me.

I'm fifty-seven.

Shelly O'Keefe

I don't even remember when Kathy told me, because it didn't really shock me or anything. I think she just introduced me to Mona, and that was it. It was about a year ago.

I'd been reading about the Gay Movement, but I'd never really thought of my sister being gay. Then when she did tell me, I was real happy. She was happy, and it was the first time I'd ever seen my sister happy.

She'd had a lot of problems. She'd always wanted to be loved by a man, or she thought she did, and they shut her down all the time. Finally she was celibate for a long time, and then she met Mona. I think it took a lot for her to admit that made her comfortable. She wasn't sure for a while; it was like she was testing it. There're only two ways to go if you want love. You've got to get it from a man or a woman. You can't have too heavy a relationship with a dog. It turned out that's where Kathy is, that's what she wants, and it's neat.

The first time I went up to Kathy and Mona's, they took me to a gay bar. I thought, "Well, what am I going to walk into?" First Kathy and Mona were dancing, then Mona and I started dancing. A woman came up to me and asked me if I wanted to dance. I wanted to tell her, "Hey, I'm not gay." It was really funny, because I just didn't know what to say or how to handle myself at that point. Mona sensed my feelings and said, "We're leaving anyway." It felt peculiar to be confronted that way by a stranger.

Knowing that Kathy's gay has made me more aware that there are people around me every day who are gay and who are happy. I can associate with them, and it pleases them that I can relate to them. They say, "What happened? How come you can accept me?" I don't have any explanation for why I understand it.

My mom has a friend who's been homosexual for as long as I've known him, and that's ten to fifteen years. I've always thought he was neat. I'm one of those people who believe if somebody's happy doing whatever they want to do, that's great. I love to see people happy.

All my friends at work are still grilling me, "How can you accept it?" I told them about Kathy because someday these people might meet my sister. If Mona's with her, they're not going to walk around staying away from each other. I like to prepare people for things, because I like to make sure people aren't going to be shocked. There are so many people who feel threatened, who think if my sister looks at one of my girlfriends, she's got the hots for her. And I'm trying to say, "No, no, no. My sister's not that way."

Most people just don't have any idea. From what they've read and from what their parents have told them, lesbians are sick people who need help. I feel it's the other way around. I don't feel my sister needs any help at all.

One girlfriend at work will say something to the effect that maybe it's rubbing off on me, because I don't shave under my arms and I don't shave my legs. She sees that as something masculine. I laugh. I think it's hilarious.

Another friend has a cousin who is gay, and she's under the impression he's going to snap out of it, that it's a passing phase. I'm trying to get her to realize that maybe this is what he wants, this is what's in him.

I'm up for anything. If I understand it well enough, and I see too many people who don't understand it or who are frightened by it, I want to help them become aware that it's here to stay and it's always been here. I try to make them understand that gay people are human; they're just like anyone else. They love; they hurt; they bleed. They just love the same sex.

It's pretty ironic, when you stop and think about all the crazy people running around. They'll accept somebody who's murdered somebody, but they can't accept somebody who is gay. I'm just going to let people know you can't go around condemning anybody for anything that's not hurting another person.

I've got my sister to thank for setting my head straight. We were never very close, because she was studious and I was always running around getting loaded, being a hippie, getting pregnant, getting abortions, doing all kinds of horrible little things that little sisters always end up doing, I guess. But her beliefs are strong in women. I used to think women were weak. But I'm strong. And my mother's strong, and my sister's strong. She helped me believe that, hey, women are out here, we're going to get out and we're going to let people know where we're at, what we want, what we're doing.

That's where I am. Nobody's going to stick me in a corner. Nobody's going to get me sitting at a desk typing, either. I'm going to make a mark on this world before I go. I'll do something. I don't know what it is, but someday I'll do it. And I'll have my sister to thank for getting the ball rolling.

I'm twenty-two.

Children

Lesbians who have children have an added set of complex decisions to face. Do you discuss your lifestyle with your children? If so, when and how? Can the children's father know, or will he then want custody? How will your lifestyle affect your children?

You will meet two new lesbian mothers in this chapter: Jean Freeperson, a fifty-year-old mother, and Sarah Megan, a twenty-two-year-old mother.

Laverne Jefferson

Tommy is only six, but he knows all about it. I told him, "A homosexual or a lesbian is someone who likes the same sex. Just because I do it, don't mean that you have to do it; you can do whatever you want to do when you get big." He goes, "I'm going to have me lots of girlfriends." I go, "Good.

Whatever you want. But I'm going to do what I want to do, huh?" And he goes, "Yeah." That's not hard for him to deal with.

He knew years and years ago, from the time he was three or four. Plenty of times he just walked in the bedroom, and I had to explain that. He'd say, "Sherry's your girlfriend, huh?" I'd say, "Yeah," and that was that. Sometimes he'd ask me things, but he hasn't for a while. I guess he knows enough now, until something new comes up on him.

At first I was worried they'd take Tommy away, but now they can't take your child away for that homosexual stuff. You used to could go to jail for being a homosexual. Now they've passed a law that as long as it's two consenting adults, it's all right.

When the laws were like that, I used to explain it just like I explained marijuana. Every once in a while, I'd give him a hit of marijuana, and I'd say, "Look, this is against the law. If you tell anybody, I'm going to jail, and you're going to jail, and then you're going to a foster home. So you can't tell different people. You can tell people that you see smoking weed." Tommy goes, "I don't want to go to jail, and I don't want you to go to jail, either." So that's how I explained it to him about being a lesbian: "Some people don't like it, and I can go to jail for it. They will take you away, and I won't be able to see you for a while; so you can't tell everybody." He goes, "You mean the pigs?" I go, "Yeah, and the social workers." He goes, "Okay." He's very bright.

My social workers and my parole officer know, and they don't bother me. When I came out of jail, I came out with my file. They'd write H or CB on it—Homosexual or Chick Business. That was on the file in red. So they all knew. My social worker is still trying to say, "You know the lady that you were with? I know Tommy grew up with her and all, so it would be good if you could get her to watch Tommy for a while."

Tommy's father and I never talked about it, but I never heard him talking bad about gay people. He's white and New Mexico Indian. Coming from a little town, he used to get so many hassles when he took Tom with him—for him being white and Tommy being Black—that I don't think he would ever ask for custody. I really don't. His family was bad enough about it. They kept saying, "That's not his, that's not his." And he'd say, "That is mine, that is mine."

I'm not worried about him growing up without a father, because I have a lot of brothers and they deal with him a lot. Sometimes he says he don't like his father. He used to say, "I want to go see my father." Then, at one point, he started saying, "I don't want to go." So I didn't tell him he had to go. And he just don't go anymore. He don't want to, so he don't have to."

Dolores Rodriguez

My lover has a child. He's three. I've been with her since he was a year old. Now that he's getting older and he's starting to be aware of things, our relationship has been rocky, because she's getting insecure. I'm getting insecure, too, because I don't know how he's going to react to everything.

I'm thinking also, "Am I really that sincere in this relationship where I'm going to affect this child's life?" He already knows that I'm a woman. He sees me and his mother sleeping together and the role-playing that's going on. I'm the one hollering at him and putting him in his room when he's bad. In another year or two, he's going to be reacting to me.

I think my lover's thinking, "I'm going to have to do it on my own: make him aware of what lesbianism is." So I moved out and now I just bring him here for a weekend, or I go down there and spend a couple of days. We're not hiding it, but I'm not there all the time and I quit doing those certain roles. She's doing everything now. I'm just there. "I've come to see you, play with you, take you to the store, take you to the park." He's going to know who I am and what I am to his mother, but I just don't want to put my role into a trip with him. I want her to raise him.

His father still comes and sees him. They were never married, so he knows that taking the child away would be impossible. She told him about our relationship. The first night I met him, he said, "You two are tripping together, huh?" I said, "Yes." He said, "Well, I'd better not ever catch you out on the streets because I'll kill you." But then he started coming over and watching TV with us and playing with the kid.

At first it was nice, but we got into a hassle, and then I didn't want him coming over no more. He wasn't coming to see Paul because he wanted to see Paul. He was depending on Paul. He'd come over drunk and grab him and hold him in his arms and fall asleep on the couch. And here I had to sit down and put up with it. So I told him, "Look, you just can't be coming over here for your own benefit. You're not coming over here to see him."

I could see it if he was coming and bringing her money or groceries for Paul, or taking Paul to the show or for a ride. Then I could see him coming over almost every day. But he was coming over for a whole other reason.

So that's when we started hassling. I told him off, and I told him why. He knew that I could see right through him, and he knew I was opening her eyes, too.

I was telling her, "You don't need him. You don't need him for that. If you really do think you need a male father image for Paul, then you need a man that's strong. Isn't that the whole trip?" She thought Paul needed to see a man around. That's when a lot of problems started, because I told her he doesn't need to see a man. I was raised without a father, and look at me—I'm fine.

She told me she could see that Paul loved me more than he loved his father. He has more respect for me. His father will come over and say, "You want to come spend the weekend with me?" And Paul will say, "No. I don't want to go." But if I come and say, "Let's go," he's ready. He's got his nightcase and his robe, "Let's go."

She wants Paul to know his father's side of the family, also, because she was adopted and she doesn't have no family. She wants him to grow up with his cousins and aunts and uncles and grandmother and grandfather. They love that little boy. He's got a lot of love.

Carol Gay

I don't think I ever told my daughter point-blank that I'm a lesbian, but I don't keep things from her. I was divorced when Crystal was four, so for the past seven years it has been just the two of us. My lifestyle's never been a secret—from the time I was a hippie doing drugs all the way through when I was hating men. She has seen the complete change.

She loved the women I was hanging out with in Mobile. She loved me hanging out with women, and she loved being with us, so the transition for her was easy. They would give her attention and a whole lot of other mothering at the same time.

My ex-husband is real straight and conservative. I used to worry about him taking Crystal away from me if he found out, but lately that fear is going away. It's not very hard to keep it from him, because he's three thousand miles away and he doesn't come to visit. Crystal visits there, but kids always know what to mention and what not to mention. She understands that a lot of people are prejudiced against lesbians.

My mother questioned my daughter on homosexuals, trying to ascertain if I was. Crystal kind of skirted the issue. She told the truth, but she didn't say anything direct. If my mother knew I was a lesbian, I think she'd be worried about custody of Crystal. Having all the old stereotypes, she'd think Crystal shouldn't grow up in this atmosphere. She could accept my being a lesbian, but she'd think, "The child is too young to know what's going on and shouldn't be there. Maybe somebody else should have Crystal."

Crystal likes my lifestyle. For the seven years that I've been divorced, she's been in a stimulating lifestyle of one sort or the other, and she says she'd be bored if she went back to being a suburban kid. She can visit her father for a month, but she doesn't want to live there. The older she gets and the more she knows her mind, the better I feel about it.

It's been just since she was eight that we've been hanging out only with women. For the last three years, she's had almost no exposure to men whatsoever, and sometimes I worry that she's getting a little too much overexposure to lesbianism. I try to counterbalance it by telling her, "It's okay. You fall in love with whoever you fall in love with, male or female. I just trust that you're going to fall in love with a really good person." A lot of my feelings are, "How could a good person be a man?" but I try to balance it out. She knows all about feminism and male chauvinism. She's grown up with the whole deal being said around her. So she has all the information, and I trust her to make her own decision later.

Vera Freeman

Even though I knew I was gay, I stayed with my husband because I thought my kids might be taken away from me. I figured the only way I could keep them was to stay with him.

Finally, I went to several agencies and found out they had to prove you were an unfit mother first, and so I decided, "Well, I won't be an unfit mother."

I also thought no one would be able to find out I was gay. I talked to a lawyer who said, "Those things are pretty hard to prove unless somebody has lots of money and ways to get an infrared camera. They've got to have you in the act."

I never directly told my husband, but by all indications, he knew, anyway. Once I went out and I didn't tell him where I was going or who I was going to be with, so he called all the women that I was going out with. When I wasn't any of those places, he got really vicious. When I came in, he asked me where I had been, and after I told him, he said, "If I ever catch you with a guy, I'll kill you. I don't mind you being with women, but I don't ever want to catch you with a guy."

He even let one of the women move in with me, us. I think he liked the woman. I think he liked the idea of my being that way. In a sense, he'd been sanctioning this all along.

One time he said, "You two are lovers," or something like that. I said, "What are you talking about?" It was just one of those little childish games where he would ask me and I would come back with something else. I'd never give in to his question because I was afraid to.

We became friends after I left, and he had the kids sometimes. When I went into the hospital with an ulcer, he kept the kids and brought them back when I came out. He brought them to see me every day at the hospital. He's nice and friendly, but I still don't want to answer that question.

He wants me to have the kids because he figures I'm going to do the best job of raising them. He told me I've done a great job with the kids. I said, "Are you ever going to try to take these kids away from me because I live with somebody?" He said, "No."

The older kids know I'm gay. I never told them directly, except for Will. I probably wouldn't have told Will, except he overheard a conversation with a gay friend of mine. I got all hot and prickly skin. I was scared. I asked him, "What do you think of your mother being a homosexual?" He said, "Well, Mom, I'd rather you gave up cigarettes than give that up."

I think he knew before that conversation. In fact, when he was nine, my roommate was saying something about homosexuality, and Will said, "Oh, I know that word." She said, "Where did you get that word from?" He said, "My dictionary." She said to me, "Why don't you take that dictionary away from that boy?" He was reading the whole dictionary, finding out what everything meant.

One time I had a pretty bad upset with a roommate. Some of the kids were living in New Orleans, and some were living here with me. My daughter here called the other kids in New Orleans and reported that I was upset, and that maybe it was due to my having an argument the night before with my friend. My son called me from New Orleans as the spokesman for the group and said, "Was that the reason?"

Of course, I denied everything. He said, "We have formed our own opinions and you can deny it if you like, but we feel that it was due to the argument with your friend there." I said, "Well, I guess you're welcome to your opinion, but that's not the case." So he said, "Well, that's the way we feel, and nobody's worth going to those extremes." I think he meant, "Be it male or female, no person is worth your destroying yourself."

None of the kids has ever said anything about my being gay, but I think they feel, "She's not making any scenes, she's not demonstrative. She's going about it in a real ladylike manner. She doesn't jump up and down in the middle of the street, so why not let her have at it?"

My roommate and I don't do a lot of touching in front

of the kids. That may be something that would embarrass them, especially my fourteen-year-old. I figure if they're going to respect me, I should respect them. They're gone enough. We have plenty of time to be together. We have our own room that we can close up into. Maybe we don't get to be close as much as we would like to, but our time comes.

Sometimes I feel quite deprived, but it's not due to the two little ones who live here. It's more due to the older ones who come around. I feel like they're intruding. My son's in the air force, and he really likes coming and bringing all of his friends. You get five tall kids in this living room and there is no room for you.

Jacqueline Denton

I knew I was going to tell my daughter Kathryn, and definitely I was going to tell Lucy, my younger daughter, but not my son because he doesn't even like people with beards. He's very, very straight. He's only now just beginning to see that's there's a possibility of having a relationship with a woman without being married to her. He's really a pathetic man. He's dull and unaware of himself and domineering. In the process of trying to make a good marriage, I damn near ruined my son because I unconsciously used him as a pawn. You know, if I could only get my son to be what his father liked, then everything would be all right. Naturally, I couldn't get him to be what his father would like.

Anyway, I think he's uninterested enough in other people that he won't notice. I have told him, of course, that I'm playing softball. Everybody thinks that's hilarious. I play kind of a right field. I usually need some backup support. My grandchildren just gave me a couple of really good workouts, so that now I catch the ball much better. I always could at least hit the ball, but not far, so I'm a good sacrifice hitter. Isn't it wonderful?

I told my daughter Kathryn when she and two-thirds of her very large family were camping on a lake in New Hampshire. She wanted me to come up and visit them at that time, so I did. I was looking for a time when there could be some kind of privacy for us. She decided the first evening she'd like to walk down from the campsite to the public telephone, so I just plain took the opportunity. I said I wanted very much to tell her this because it was important to me. I said, "The softball team is more important than it sounds, because actually I'm in love with one of the players on the team, a woman named Sandra."

Kathryn has been getting more and more liberal in her Catholicism in recent years, and I think she wants to be considered a broadminded person, so she was listening respectfully and interestedly. We got interrupted almost immediately after I'd had a chance to tell her something about Sandra, so it got put off to the next day.

When we had a minute or two, I said, "Does what I'm talking about upset you?" She said, "Upset me? Why?" I said, "Well, it is rather unconventional." She said, "Ha! If I should be upset at everything unconventional I have to put up with, I would never have a quiet moment."

One day before I left the lake, everybody scattered to the four winds. Some were going fishing; some were going into the village; some were going swimming. Kathryn and I were literally left alone in the campsite, which was a miracle. There were more than eighteen people on the two campsites, what with friends and children.

I said, "I want to know how you feel about what I told you, about me and Sandra." She started a kind of philosophical discussion and said, "New experiences are really good, but they should all be based on absolutely solid ground." I knew she was saying that, for her, the solid ground was her faith. She was challenging me to say what my solid ground was, or to prove that in some way I had a solid ground. She went on doing quite a lot of philosophical development of a theme. Then she said, "Well, of course, with existential angers, we always have to find something to attach them to."

I said, "Kathryn, this doesn't make any sense to me. I'd like you to be more specific." She went back to the same business—that an experience has its qualities depending upon the firm ground on which it's based. I said this was a very important experience to me, and I felt it could meet any of the criteria she might want to put up.

I was scared when I was talking with her, but I had to be in real control. I was being cool and thinking over what she was saying, but I did not understand what she was doing philosophically. That could have been because I was nervous and couldn't maintain concentration.

I said, "We have to be more specific. I want to know how you would feel if I were here with Sandra." She said, "I'd feel all right." I said, "Well, suppose we were flamboyantly affectionate with each other?" She said, "I could always ask you to leave my campsite." I said, "This also could be important enough to me so that I would be getting political about it. I could appear at a pro-abortion rally or for gay rights." She said, "Well, depending on the circumstances, I'd have to reconsider our relationship."

She was cool as a cucumber. She's in control of herself, this woman is. I think she meant she would protect herself and her family and that maybe I wouldn't be so welcome when all the kids were around. She's a very powerful woman and so am I, so I was not going to be particularly kind to her. I was not going to say I wouldn't do any of these things. I said, "It's good for me to know where you stand, and I certainly will take all you've said into consideration."

Later, we were winding things up in a more comfortable way, and I knew it was time for me to leave. I said, "Just one more thing. If you are worried about me, under no circumstances should you hesitate to call me, because we can always talk." She said, "Worry about you? Of course not. I don't ever worry about you. When friends of mine say to me, 'Aren't you worried with your mother going off to the Himalayas?' I always say, 'Oh, no. I can't imagine anything more magnificent or appropriate than if she should fall off an Alpine peak or a Himalayan cliff.' " That's what she said! Of course, I have been in the Himalayas and I have been on Alpine peaks, but only the low peaks.

For a while, I worried that our talk might interfere with our intimacy. But then she called me on the telephone to tell me about the various things she was setting up for herself during her work year and the time she'd be taking off. She said, "Save the weekend in January for my regular recreation thing. I'm going to take a long one, this time. I'll probably come to your place on a Tuesday evening and not go home until Monday."

We had many telephone conversations before I started West for a recent conference. She was very relaxed, very natural, very comfortable. She may be accommodating herself to this in some kind of a way. She really does want to be broadminded. She's fifty. She was a bigoted Catholic before she went back to college. She went to college for seven and a half years and became an occupational therapist when she was forty-nine.

Lucy, my second daughter, was much easier. She's almost forty-three, and she's been in a much more liberal and experimental environment. She taught for seven years in a highly innovative high school; she left her first husband, married again, and had to fight for custody of the children. I've supported her in many difficult situations. Indeed, I would not, under any circumstance, let her down in any way. What she does I can disapprove, but I'm supporting her in every way I can.

I told her very soon after I got to her home in Colorado. This was just ten days before I came here to the conference. I said, "One of the things I want to tell you about is that I am involved with a woman. In fact, I'm in love with her, and she's in love with me." "Oh, that's great. You must tell Carol about it," says she.

She has two pretty grown-up daughters: Amy, who's finished two years at Harvard, and Carol, who's starting her second year of college. Lucy and the two girls have always talked about everything under the sun, including love affairs and masturbation.

Lucy asked me a lot of questions which I was happy to answer and said she was aware of how hungry I have always been. I was feeling just great. I'd had a fantasy that I would really be able to talk with Lucy about anything: about all aspects of my relationship, the funny jokes, the gay bars, the jealousies. I did talk somewhat about it, but I could talk quite a lot more about it with Carol, because one of Carol's very best friends from high school has realized that she's lesbian. This was a problem for Carol, and she really needed to talk with me about it. Carol is nineteen.

Amy was immediately interested when she came. She is the oldest grandchild, the one who is going to Harvard. When I talked over the telephone with Sandra, Amy was interested in what kind of things were going on. Amy and I were really exchanging confidences; she would tell me about her various difficulties with men.

The interesting thing was that from the time the girls were there, if I started to talk with Lucy about Sandra, she changed the subject. It was very obvious to me that Lucy was no longer interested. When I was talking, she wouldn't answer—that's a trick she's used for years. Then I would feel unanswered and drop it; or if I went on, she'd say, "Did you want to cut up some more peaches?"

She told me later on that she and Kathryn had talked

about me on the telephone when I was off with one of the kids. She wouldn't tell me what Kathryn said, but she told me what she said. "I see it the same as when you got so interested in the groups, and like your enthusiasm about the man two years ago which didn't last very long. Now you're enthused about the softball team and Sandra. You get energized and have a big investment in these things, and they're really good for you." It was as if she were saying, "But I don't expect it to last." I'm capable of real loyalty, but she doesn't know it.

She was also disengaging herself from being very much concerned about what I was doing, because she went on with, "Oh, this is so fascinating. I wonder how the increase in lesbianism is going to influence the human species." She's a biologist. I said, "It is very important that some lesbian women want to have children, but they want to have them without the intervention of a man." She said, "Well, of course, that's possible. It will be very interesting to see what happens to the gene pool."

Tonya Holloway

Daniel was definitely a planned child. I had a relationship with a man deliberately to have a kid. I chose the father according to what I wanted out of a man for a kid. I told him, "Look, I want to get pregnant, and if you don't do it, I'll just go out and find somebody else who will." So he did. As soon as I missed a period three days, I came back home from Hawaii because I knew I was pregnant. There was no way in hell I was going to stay over there with the guy.

When I realized I was a lesbian, the first thing I worried about was, "Is this going to affect my son?" He was two, and it was very important to me that he have a decent upbringing. I had the whole horror story in my mind of this poor kid not having any male images and turning out to be crazy.

Even though Daniel hadn't had a male image before I took the label of lesbian, it was like, "Wow, is this going to mess him up?" I finally realized that whatever men I did have in my life would be good men, the type of male image I wanted. I decided, "It's not like my taking this label will automatically make him grow up to be a murderer, or something. In fact, my lifestyle now is better because I don't have weird men walking in and out of my house all hours of the night. He's got a more stable life this way."

I also worried, "What if I'm in a relationship with a woman and one of his friends starts coming around going, 'Your mother's a lesbian. Your mother's a lesbian'?" Kids can be really cruel. But then I thought, "It would be the same thing as them saying, 'You're wearing glasses. You're wearing glasses.'" If some kid ran around saying, "Your mother's a lesbian," he could say, "Well, so what? Your mother's a heterosexual." By that point, my relationships would be happy and fulfilling, so that he wouldn't think it was bad to be a lesbian.

What's strange is that people don't think you're a lesbian if you have a kid. They think you're really normal. "Well, she already knows the joys of motherhoood, and this man sort of messed her up so she's staying away from men for a while, but she's still had a man so that means she's okay." Nobody ever thinks weird things about me having so many women friends or women's barbecues because I have a son. In a way, it's a lot easier than being a totally single person with no kid.

Jean Freeperson

I realized I was a lesbian five years ago when I was forty-five years old. One of my biggest terrors was that if my twenty-six-year-old son found out I was gay, he would reject me. He lives in the same city I do.

Already, gay life is so hard, but it's even harder at fifty
years old and living in this town. I thought, "If I lose my son
over this, I just don't know what I'll do. I need him in my
life." Well, that was obviously a paranoid fantasy, because
I hadn't raised him to be that way.

What I did was I showed him my lifestyle little by little
and let him draw his own conclusions. My lover would talk
to him about it in a very subtle way. She'd say, "You know
how much I love your mother, and we're not getting along.
I wish that I could stay with her always." Things like that
are rather innocuous, but they can be taken on two levels.

I'm sure he went through a lot of agony, but he finally
came into the realization. He showed me that he knew in the
most wonderful way possible. He simply started talking
about a mutual friend of ours who is gay and said, "Blah,
blah, blah, and he's gay, too, Mom." That little word "too"
just did the whole thing. We didn't have to have a confron-
tation. I didn't have to sit down and tell him my life's story.

I do want to talk to him sometime soon, though. I'm sure
he must look back on his young life and wonder if I was sleeping around with women. I want to get that straight with him,
because I don't want to invalidate his childhood. I don't want
him to think, "Gee, I saw Mom with her arm around somebody when I was five or six years old; I wonder what was
going on." I really want to get it clear that his childhood
wasn't a dishonest lie.

My daughter is twenty-one years old, and she's up in Mon-
tana. It hasn't been right to try to tell her because there's
been too much instability in her life. I'm not afraid of losing
her love. She's just been such a confused person, and people
close to me have agreed with this. "Don't tell Cheryl now; it
would blow her away."

I'm fifty, and I was born and raised in Kent, Ohio, an

upper-middle-class university town. I was an airline stew-
ardess for two years. I was married for twenty years, have two
children, twenty-one and twenty-six. I'm white, and I'm a
recovered alcoholic. I have a B.A. and a master's in education. I've taught every level, from kindergarten through
graduate school. I've been a dean of girls at a high school, a
vice-principal of an elementary school, and an administrator
in the district schools office. It has been a heavy identity
change from being a completely heterosexual woman, with
the plastic hair and fingernail polish, to the screaming dyke
you see here before you.

Sarah Megan

I've considered myself a lesbian for the past six months,
and my main worry has been that my child's father, Ivan,
doesn't find out. We went through a year and a half of real
heavy court hassles when we were divorcing. He tried to
contest custody, and he's been really weird. He tried to hit
me with a car; he broke windows; he ripped off my distribu-
tor cap when he saw my car parked in different places.

Ivan didn't want to split up, so it took him a good year
or more to get his own life together and feel good about
himself. Now he's relating to another woman, but I still
don't trust him. When he would kick into this weird space,
it would be totally unlike him, and I couldn't reach him. I
don't want him to start threatening me again and want his
son. He's very close to Zachary, and he thinks he knows
what's right and wrong for him.

I think, at this point, Ivan feels like he couldn't give Zack
the environment and the school I'm giving him now, but at
the same time, if he wanted to get nasty, he could use my
being a lesbian against me. There're women losing their
children all the time because they're lesbians.

I see Ivan sometimes every weekend, sometimes once every two months. It depends if his car is running. He comes and gets Zachary.

He knows one of my housemates is gay. When we talked about it, he wasn't real down on it, as I remember. He said, "Whatever people feel they want to do." But I know when it would get down to a gut level of his son and his ex-wife, it would probably be a different story.

He's been around my lover lots of times; he's talked to her for hours, sometimes. Paula and I don't hold hands, we don't touch each other when he's around.

Zachary's two and a half, and pretty soon he might start saying things. Sometimes he wakes up in the morning, and before he even knows what's going on he says, "Hi, Sarah, hi, Paula," and Paula may not even be in my bed. Sometime Ivan might ask Zack, "Who does Sarah kiss?" That's a possibility. I just avoid the subject.

It's important to me to raise the two children I live with in a nonsexist manner, where they see women as women can be. I'm really getting off on raising a son. I would get off on raising a girl, too, but I think it's far out for Zack to have contact with strong women.

With all the friends I have with their different lifestyles, Zachary's going to be able to see a little bit of everything. I just think it's real important to offer a lot of alternatives and not isolate the child into one way of living life.

I was born in Santa Barbara into an upper-middle-class family, and I graduated from high school when I was sixteen. I went to college in music for two years, but I was real disappointed in the program. So I dropped out and worked in a plant nursery, then as a motel maid, then in the orange groves.

I met Ivan when I was eighteen or nineteen. I'm twenty-

two now. I didn't really want to get married, but I got pregnant, and he said that if I had an abortion, he didn't want
to relate with me anymore. So we got married, then split up,
and I moved into a collective on a farm. It felt real isolated,
and I knew I wanted to go back to school so I wouldn't have
to be on welfare for the next six years. I got into auto mechanics and machine shop, and now I'm an auto mechanic,
which I love.

Within Our Institutions
School and Work

Most of us spend a good part of our waking hours in school or at work. Our relationships with schoolmates, teachers, co-workers, employees, and employers can determine whether those hours are pleasant or miserable. Do co-workers and schoolmates need to know you are a lesbian? How do you tell them or keep it from them? Will you get fired or ostracized if people find out?

Everyone but Jackie and Canyon had something to say about school or work. Jackie just said, "I'm retired. My loyalty to the school I worked at for twenty-four years is very strong. I would not want to mess anything up for them, so I wouldn't talk about it with them."

In this chapter you will meet a lesbian administrator, Lea Cross, who will share her strategies for dealing with harassment on the job.

Carol Queen

I'm working right now as a clerk. I'm trying to get money together to go back to school because I declared myself financially independent from my parents about a year ago.

I'm accepted at work, which is a neat thing. All the people I work with know, and none of them seem to care. Telling them just came naturally. Some are people I had known before, and before I was hired, I told my boss. When I was having the initial interview, I said, "I want to know how open you are. If you see my name on the front page of the paper, are you going to fire me?" He said, "Not if you do your work." So I was lucky.

For a while, I was working as a waitress for a real red-neck. He is one of the organizers of a group in town called the Taxpayers' League, or something. It's very Mom and apple pie. The guy who is the president of it used to come in and eat all the time. He never tipped me, and he always wore his hard hat, which I thought was just symbolic as anything. I was real paranoid about that. Every time I walked past that guy, I felt like he was about to hit me with a hard hat or a hammer or God knows what else.

I figured if anything happened in the media when I was still working there, I would just face the music and say, "Okay, fire me. So what." It worked out pretty well because I hated the job and quit before my name got in the paper.

Laverne Jefferson

I was gay when I was still going to high school. I had some friends that I told and they dealt with it, but then they started flashing on me. My close friends would tease me and

say, "Hey, babe," and I'd say, "You'd better stop." Then I
quit school, and that was that. I went to continuation school
because I just couldn't deal with the system.

At one point, I was teaching physical education in elementary school. I'd wear this green sweatsuit, and the little
kids would say, "Are you a girl or a boy?" The female
teachers said, "You should try to uphold a feminine image."
I said, "Have you ever tried to teach P.E. in a dress?" The
two male teachers would stick up for me and say, "Yeah, I
haven't seen a P.E. teacher in a dress, either." So that was
that.

But then I would hear the other teachers say, "I think
Laverne's a homosexual," and I wouldn't say anything. I
can't remember whether they called it queer or lesbian, but
they were referring to being gay. Me and the sixth grade
teacher had gotten really close because she seen all the hell
I got for being a minority. They'd say that me and the
sixth grade teacher had something going because we were
always together, but the sixth grade teacher didn't even
know I was gay.

Finally, I quit. If they had known I was gay, I would
have lost my job, anyway. They would have said I was seducing the little girls, or something.

Jeri

I'm an accountant. I used to be a pretty bad closet case.
I was mindful of every word I said, so that nobody would
look and see what I was. When I first started living with
Rose, I even went so far as to make up a fictional boyfriend
at work. I soon found out that was not very comfortable, so
the next job I dropped him. I had to carry him for two
years, and he got awfully boring.

I've gradually worked up to the point that now I'm very

vocal about my feelings on life, although I don't say I'm gay. In the lunchroom we talk about things that affect gay people's lives. I consider myself a feminist first, and I have been busy raising the consciousness of the men and women I work with. In that context, I do a little educating as far as gay lifestyles go. Whenever there's an article in the paper, I bring it to their attention, and we discuss it.

I'm very relaxed about who I am at work. I'm fortunate that I'm the only woman executive in the company, and I have a very good future in the executive program. I've even had thoughts of going in to see my boss, closing the door, and saying, "I've got something I want to share with you, something that's really neat in my life, and I'd just like you to know about it."

There's enough about me they pick up that they might know, anyhow. I talk about Rose all the time. In fact, I'm going to take her to the Christmas party this year. It's going to blow their minds, and I'm going to love it. We will not dance together. They're not ready for that.

Maria Gonzales

After my babysitter brought me out when I was seven, I started turning on all the little girls my age, doing it in back of the school closet. In South Carolina, there was this watch-tower the kids could play at that was used for fire watches for the town. After school, during recess, during lunch, I would have some little girl up there. It didn't have to be the same one all the time. I was showing them all the amazing things this other girl had shown me.

When I was in sixth grade, I was in Girl Scouts. There must have been about fifteen girls in there, and I did it with every single one of them.

When I hit junior high, I met two other dykes who were baby butches, too. We were like a trio, stomping around, causing uproars all over the school. We didn't realize all the girls in junior high school would do it with us just in order to be our friends. That hurt, after one point. I didn't realize that my lover was being my lover just because she was afraid that if she wasn't my lover, we wouldn't be friends. But before that, I was really hot. We were all hot to trot.

On the other hand, there were some girls, officers' kids, who would pull rank on me and say, "Do it with me." I would say, "You don't really turn me on. I'm not into that kind of a trip. You can't just come and power-play me." They'd say, "Do it to me or I'll say you did, and then you'll be in a lot of trouble." So I ended up doing it with some real weird people.

When my friend's mother caught my friend and me doing it in the back of her station wagon, the principal of the school found out, and he beat the shit out of me. He said, "Well, you know, you're just looking at the girls too much lately." He bent me over and wet the paddle and really let me have it. That was in seventh grade, and from seventh through ninth grade, he was on my case really heavy.

If I would drop a pencil on the floor in class and I would bend down to pick it up, one of my teachers would go, "All right, Gonzales, are you so interested in so-and-so's legs that you can't pay attention to the class?" I dropped my pencil once in science class, and he kicked me out of the class for six weeks.

In this one class, though, our teacher was very, very loose. There were about four of us who were butches, and we all had our girlfriends, and we'd make out in the back of the class.

At one point, I was going steady with this guy because a friend of mine said it would put off some pressure. We never even kissed. He would ask me to go to the movies, and I would ask my girlfriend to go, and we'd all go together.

When other girls would go with their boyfriends, I would sit next to them. I would put my arm around this girl, and her boyfriend would look at me weird, and he'd put his arm on top of mine, and I'd put my arm on top of his. We'd do this whole thing, and then I'd go home with her. The boys were pissed. None of the girls—except for maybe one that I knew of—was balling because all the other girls would take them home at night, and we'd call up our parents and say, "I'm spending the night at Susan's house."

Sometimes I would get really dressed up to go to a school dance, and I'd dance with all these other girls. Then, before I left the dance, I would take off my dress, put on one of my brother's red blazers and a pair of black pants, and I would take somebody home or go home with somebody.

When I came to California to high school, it was very strained because I wasn't on base anymore, and I was very lonely. I only did it with one or two people in high school, and that's when the heaviness came down. Everybody else was coming out of puberty and identifying with their sex, except for me, or so I thought.

I felt no qualms about it for a long time until I told my best friend, and she jumped out of my moving car. That's when I started realizing that there's something wrong in being gay to a lot of people. It was really weird. I said, "You're going to give me a heart attack. Get back in this car." She said, "No." I said, "What's the matter with you? You've known me for three years. All of a sudden, you're jumping out of a car. I haven't done nothing to you in three years. What is your trip?" So we talked about it, and she said, "That's true. I'm just really freaked out." I said, "Well, how do you think I feel, with you jumping out of a moving car because I tell you that I am a lesbian? I didn't realize you

were going to take it that hard." And then another friend
of mine didn't take it that bad. But she wouldn't talk to me.
There was a definite strain.

By my junior year, whoever was going to hang around me
knew I was gay. A lot of the women said, "Oh, that's just a
phase you're going through. We all go through that. You're
just going through it a little later."

Chrystos

I've done all kinds of odd jobs within the lesbian community, so I've never been worried about coming out on
the job. I've had a fairly protected life in many senses. I
write poetry and do drawings. Lately, I've been selling a lot
of drawings, and that's how I've been making my money.

Now I'm thinking that I really need to get a job because
I'm tired of living on a ledge, scrabbling around from day
to day. I've been thinking a lot about what it would be like
to try to get back into the straight world. That's not very
appealing to me.

In most of the job discrimination I've heard women describe, nobody came right out and said, "You're queer; get
your ass out of here." It was much more this weird stuff that
you can't quite put your finger on. You just become so uncomfortable that you have to get out.

Esther Brown

Back in the fifties and sixties, I occasionally went to gay
bars, but I had to be very discreet. Being in management
for a huge oil company, I always worried that someone
would see me. I was on guard all the time because my position was at stake.

A woman who worked for me was quite infatuated with me. One night we both got plastered and had sort of a relationship. Well, that became quite difficult at the office. I lucked out, though, because her parents were trying to persuade her to go back to get her B.A., since she only had one semester left. She had ambitions of becoming a career woman in the oil company, and her parents didn't want that.

So I had a long talk with her and convinced her she should go back and get her B.A. Then, if she felt that the career plan was the one she wished, she could come back to the oil company. I figured that, in the meantime, she'd realize this was just an infatuation, which it was. She eventually ended up getting married and now has a couple of kids. Her parents were thankful that I convinced her she should go back to school, and yet I had this ulterior motive. It was just too difficult for both of us under the circumstances.

Where you work is a real factor in the time it takes you to come out. I'm sure that's what keeps many, many women from coming out, or from at least admitting it to themselves. I'm fifty-three years old, so it took a long time.

For years, I'd been planning to buy a ranch or farm. I decided, since I wanted a ranch anyway, living in the country would be the easiest way to live the life I wanted without having to account to a superior, an organization, or a company for my personal life. I was hoping I could make my entire living here on the ranch. Unfortunately, I had to start doing a paper route also, so I did deviate that much in my determination by taking a job with the local paper, which is pretty straitlaced.

But now, at least, I can live. I can admit to my sisters who I am. We can enjoy each other's company, and I no longer have to look out of the corner of my eye every day to see if someone's observing me.

Rose

In school, when I was looking for gay women, it was very difficult. You have to try to look for some of them that maybe they're not so pretty, those who don't run around with men a lot or with boys. I found one of them. I know she was gay because she was not interested in boys at all, didn't matter what shape or form. We never talked about it, but we were the best of friends. We had a real good relationship just being friends, which was great, because that was what I needed, and I'm sure that was what she needed, also.

You see, it was very difficult for me to relate an awful lot to people because I didn't know English. So it was really difficult for me trying to learn English, trying to find the kind of friends that I wanted, rather than the kind that would run around with boys a lot. So I was really having a little bit of a hard time.

This one girl told me that her mother was in the army and that there was a lot of lesbians in the army. Her mother's a real dyke, too, she really is. So I tried to go and join the army, but my parents wouldn't sign for it, so I couldn't go in. I wanted to be with all the women.

Now I do accounting work in an office which has about three hundred women. I whistle at the girls, the women. I tell them they look sexy, and I tell them they look very pretty.

I never told them I'm gay, but I never hide it. If they want to know I'm gay, I'd tell them. If they don't ask me, then I don't speak it. Jeri sends me flowers, and they ask me who they're from, and I say, "Jeri."

As a matter of fact, I whistled at a girl today. She was sitting down at her desk, combing her hair and powdering her nose. I whistled, and she says, "Who did that?" I said,

"Not me." But she knew who it was because I do that all the time. This one woman, she says, "If it were somebody else, I'd be worried, but since it's you, I expect it." So I don't have any problem at work.

Jane Salter

I haven't had any trouble at all at school because of being gay, and I have said I am gay in classes that were not women's classes. Of course, you realize I'm at U.C. Berkeley where there's a large gay student population, not to mention the staff and teachers.

I couldn't continue the regular master's in English because I couldn't stand the standard English program anymore, so I'm getting a special master's, and two women friends of mine supervise me. I couldn't stand the men teachers. They were so pompous, and I was very threatening to them because I'm articulate and extroverted and I would never call them *Mr.* So-and-so. My grades were at stake in those situations, and since my convictions have always overridden my sensibilities, I had to get out of the situation to protect myself scholastically. I was also bored to tears not reading about women.

Dolores Rodriguez

Although in school I wore dresses and skirts, I never had a boyfriend, and I never talked about boys. I would hear all the girls' stories, but I was always just a listener. What was a trip was that those girls used to hang on me and play with my ears and squeeze my cheeks and do all these weird little trips to me.

Then in high school, my emotions started growing stronger

for these women around me, and my clothes weren't like theirs. I didn't wear makeup or comb my hair a certain way. I used to wear Levi's and T-shirts, while my friends were in miniskirts and mascara. But they still always wanted me to hang around with them.

In high school, there was a couple of lesbians. I would never talk to them, but I would always watch them, and they always watched me, also: you know, walking down the hall, that eye contact. You say, "Oh, no, here comes the other one. I wonder if she knows I'm gay." Finally, I just started talking to them. They're the ones who introduced me to my first lover.

Where I work right now is partly gay. My boss, who owns the business, is gay, and some of the assemblers are gay. We have one man who is going to have surgery and change into a woman. So that atmosphere right there is helping me out because I can work a decent job and get along with my supervisors without having that fear.

Another lesbian told me about this job. I went and applied, and they hired me. I didn't tell them I was gay, but they knew because I was her friend. She looks like a man, but you know she's a woman because of her breasts. They probably thought I was her lover, so they hired me.

Carol Gay

Work was no problem. I had started my own clothing business in Mobile with a friend, so I didn't have anybody to report to, and I didn't have to deal with employees or anyone. My gay friends from the bar were welcome in my store all the time. A couple of them worked down the street, and we'd all go out for lunches together. It was like this fantasy world; nothing else existed but us.

Vera Freeman

I'm not frightened, but I wouldn't go on my job and say, "This is what I do." If I did, I might not have the money to support these kids. I like tax auditing, and I don't want to get blackballed. I don't want that to go down on my record.

You see, I don't even know what happens when people know you are gay. I've never admitted it to anyone, other than gay people or my close friends. So I don't know what would happen.

I wear suits to work, and sometimes I wear dresses. The only thing about me is my short hair, and I wear earrings. Do I look like a lesbian? Besides, I've got eight kids and I'm forty-five, so they figure I'm over the hill.

I don't talk about my personal life. I wouldn't talk about my personal life if I were living with a dude. I sometimes mention my roommate, and they know she's a female. Several of them have met her. I guess people just accept me as I am.

Some of the guys did ask me, "Do you ever go out with guys?" I said, "Yes," because I did. I went out with guys. But I wasn't going to talk about my personal experiences.

One of the reasons women are having such a hard time out there in the working world is because they expose themselves. They leave themselves open for the kind of talk that goes around about them. I've been in groups where people say about a woman: "She's really having a hard time," or, "She's a fool to stay with him." They know all about this woman's life. Well, they're not going to know about mine.

I'm not discriminated against as a lesbian because they don't know. But due to the fact that I don't discuss certain things with them, that I will walk away from certain conversations or play them down, I am discriminated against. I am considered not like them. Maybe they think it's because

I'm Black, I don't know. I have been discriminated against
for being a Black.

Mary Howland

I have a very unusual situation at work, and I think that
has to do with the fact that I'm an unusual person. I am
probably more open and take more risks and am less self-
destructive than most people I know.

When I came to work at my present nursing job, I had
just come out to myself and didn't say anything, but right
after my first lover and I got together, my hospital wooed
her there for a job. Anita had been known to be gay for
ten years by the people in the hospital, and, of course, they
hired her because of her competence. Knowing she was gay
didn't make any difference. With Anita and me moving in
together, the boss got the clue. We had our relationship in
front of the whole world practically, so within a year the
boss knew and the executive director knew.

When Anita and I broke up after eight months, I went
to my boss and said, "I'm going to have to take a week off."
She said, "What's the matter?" I said, "Anita and I have
broken up, and I'm not handling it well. I can't function
at work." She said, "It's okay. Take a week off, and when
you come back, take care of yourself. When you find you've
had as much as you can take of this place, get out and go
home." What she was doing was honoring the fact that I
had lost somebody very significant, and it was just as important as if a straight person had lost somebody through
death or divorce. It was just really, really beautiful.

In fact, the boss actually helped me and my lover. I had
to work very closely with Anita at a time when things were
so angry that she refused to admit I existed. The boss, who
is a fantastic nurse practitioner, helped us do something to

bridge that gap of anger and disappointment in a session that was four hours long.

Olivia Moreno

When I went to high school, I thought about being gay now and then, but I didn't deal with it. I was lonely, but I knew that when I was old enough, I'd move away to a town where there was gay people. That was my goal. Me and a guy were the top hoods of the school: black leather jackets, switchblades, all that kind of stuff. So people didn't ask me very many questions, and I wasn't open about it at all.

I'm completely open now at the college. Like I just wrote a paper today for an anthropology class on our personal culture, and I did it about being gay. Of course, the professor is a good friend of mine and she knows I'm gay, so it wasn't too hard for me to do.

I don't tell everybody. I don't think it's everybody's business. But I tell people I think it might concern or people I'm friends with. I told the instructor of this class and some other people that are active on campus, because I didn't want them to see me on a panel or in the Gay People's Alliance office and then be shocked because I didn't tell them.

It was really funny the other day. I was sitting in the Gay People's Alliance office, and an old high school teacher walked by. My heart started beating, and I thought, "Oh, my God." I literally crawled underneath the desk. There were four gay people in the office, and they go, "What are you doing?" I said, "That's my old high school teacher." They go, "Oh, okay." They covered up for me, but they were giving me funny looks because they know I'm really open.

Then I said, "God, I'm not going to do this for anybody." So I got up and walked over to her and said, "Hi." She was in the next office, and she was excited to see me. She said,

"What are you doing here?" I said, "Oh, I work over in the
Gay People's Alliance." She said, "Oh, really?" It blew her
away. I know she's going to go back to my old high school
and say, "Guess who I saw and where I saw her?" Shit. But
I don't care. I don't have to deal with that crowd anymore,
so it's not important. I'm not hiding.

Lea Cross

I met my first lover when she and I were administrators
at the same firm. Our jobs were sort of political in nature,
so we were vulnerable, to some extent. One of our main
concerns was that someone might use our relationship to get
either one or both of us fired, or to try to get something they
wanted from the firm.

We used a very selective coming-out-to-certain-people-we-
trust process at work. There were other gay people working
there, and I came out to some of them. My style is to plan
things out and try to prepare a proper situation to tell
people, but my lover just does it when the occasion arises.
She has told people that I have had some question about her
telling, and I know I've told people that she's had question
about my telling, but we trust one another and hope that
both of us are making good decisions.

I never have come out completely in my work situation.
I think maybe one of the hardest ways to do it is to be out
to some people and not out to other people, although it certainly has its safety aspects. To some extent, the people
you've told will protect you, and provide you with a support
group to talk to.

On the whole, I would say that the people at work have
been really cool. There were some rather uncomfortable
ones, but those were not people we told but people who
somehow found out about our relationship.

At one point, some people tried to blackmail my lover into doing something they wanted within the firm. They said, "If you don't do this, there will be dire repercussions" —the strong implication being that all of the lesbians in the firm were going to be exposed. I don't know how many millions of lesbians they thought that was going to be. Camille refused to go along with it, and evidently there was a letter circulated to the city council, but there were no direct repercussions that ever got back to us.

Then there was another situation where an employee who had decided to leave the firm, upon making that decision, wrote a letter to the funding people, saying the firm was made up primarily of homosexuals and that consequently it was a difficult working situation. That letter was widely circulated in the community. Many of the allegations that were made would have been so difficult to substantiate that it was a very ticklish situation for a while. The firm board spent a lot of time dealing with the whole thing. Some people, of course, were horrified that there might really be gay people working at the firm.

At that point, both of us sought and received legal advice on how to deal with it. We were told to maintain the position that the firm had no right to seek information about someone's private life, unless it was obvious that the person's private life was detrimental to the job. As an employer, you have to be able to show that a person's being homosexual is really going to be a detriment to performing the job.

Since that time, I've read some legal stuff that says it's still more up in the air than that. It really depends on whose court you go into, what kind of protections you have. It's much more fashionable and even politically all right in some circles to discriminate against or be prejudiced against homosexuals than it is against ethnic minorities or even women.

Anyway, it was just a lump charge, and there weren't people mentioned by name. Presumably, the person was willing to name names, but the person was asked to a hearing about the letter and never showed up. To try to substantiate the things that were in the letter would have really put the person in a difficult position from a legal standpoint. When you're accusing someone of being a homosexual, you have to have some pretty concrete knowledge that they are, and there are only a very limited number of ways to get that knowledge.

Some people who were on the board had dealt with those kinds of threats to employees previously in other firms and had recognized that you don't do a firm any good by trying to pursue that. Other members of the board were caught up in the intrigue or the juicy gossip of it. At any rate, no one got fired as a result of it, and it all just died down.

Religion

Church doctrines, interpretations of church doctrines, and opinions of the clergy on lesbianism vary greatly among religions and often within a single religion. Some women who have religious beliefs or close ties with a church find themselves in a dilemma when they realize they are lesbians; others do not. Esther, Canyon, and Jackie all said that religion was no problem for them and didn't elaborate. Other women had stories to tell.

In this chapter, you will meet a new woman and her mother, Theresa and Elizabeth Reilly, who found themselves facing the disapproval of the Mormon church.

Carol Queen

I didn't need to deal with religion, because I dealt with religion a long time ago. What I basically did was squash it in my own life.

For a short time when I was twelve, I was a witch. It was not just a brief flirtation with the occult. It was a need for a religion that I could control. I came up with this explanation a couple of years later, but that's what it really was.

It was all the earth spirit and matriarchal stuff, and yet I called the shots; I did the spells. I did a whole lot of easy little ones, and they all came true, so I figured, "Hey, I'm pretty good." For example one day I decided I didn't want it to snow the next day, so I did a spell, and it didn't. I was real cautious about the control I tried to exercise.

But then that need for some kind of religious base just dissolved. I think it's possibly because what I really wanted to hear was, "You can control your own destiny."

Laverne Jefferson

I still say I'm Baptist, but I don't go to church anymore. I haven't been to church in eight, nine years. When I was small, I got pushed to church so much that I couldn't stand it.

Being gay in a Black church would be pretty hard. They tell you going with the same sex is a sin. I mean they really preach it to you; they really scare you. From them pounding religion in me, I used to think about it a whole bunch, and I would worry about going to hell. But then after I did it, I just thought, "Well, I just won't go to church no more. If God had made some better men, it wouldn't have been like this." Now I figure that I'm not going to heaven or to hell, I'm going in between. It's not going to be burning, and I'm not going to have paradise.

When my mom gets drunk, she says, "Judgment day's gonna come, and God's gonna mark you for each and every thing. First of all, for being disobedient to your parents, and sinning," which, I take it, is going with the same sex. But I don't pay her any attention. I just tell her, "I got to live my life the way I want to live my life."

Jeri

I was raised in the Church of God. It's not Pentecostal, but it's very fundamental, and I had a lot of trouble dealing with that. You can't be raised in a church for eighteen years and not have some of that still inside you.

Probably the thing that helped me the most was the realization that any religious experience is a personal one. It's not the organized church or the pastor that does your religion for you. It's between you and God, you and Jesus as your personal savior. When I finally realized that I didn't have to worry about what a body of people or a human being who was my pastor might say about me, when I finally realized the thing that mattered was my relationship with God, then I didn't worry so much about the rules and the doctrines and the theology.

I thought if I really prayed to God, somehow I would get my answer. I would find peace within myself, or I would find it was not a thing I should be doing.

My answer didn't come right away. In fact, during the time that I was searching for it, Rose and I broke up for a couple of months. During that time, she happened to go to the Metropolitan Community Church, which is a church in San Francisco that primarily ministers to homosexuals. It's interdenominational. When we got back together again, she said, "I'd like to take you to this church and see what you think of it."

It was probably exactly what I needed at that time. I still hadn't quite resolved the way I felt, and it was important for me to be able just to sit down and talk to ministers: to Baptist ministers, priests, Assembly of God pastors; to people who had perhaps even been married and who had finally found out who they were; to people who had had all the same doubts and questions and discomfort that I had. To be able to sit in a church and look around and see all my brothers and sisters praising the Lord through song, praying together, and receiving communion together really helped me find that inner peace. In that respect, Metropolitan Community Church was probably the thing that helped me resolve that conflict. I wish I had found it a lot earlier.

Maria Gonzales

When I was thirteen, I confessed to a priest that I was a lesbian. I thought it was a sin so I should confess it, but he said that it was all right and that he was gay. He said, "God isn't going to condemn you. God is all good. How can he condemn something that he's made?"

Chrystos

When I was twenty-two or twenty-three, I got involved in an ashram, and I was doing meditation every morning. The man who was the leader of it was very hostile to the idea of two women being lovers. It was apparent that my lover and I were lovers, and he would say things in general during his lectures about how that was being too attached to the body. There was no way that as a lesbian I could be part of that community.

Eventually, I dropped out, very hurt and very traumatized by the fact that I couldn't love a woman according to this man and also be holy or be enlightened. Although meditation gave me an awful lot at that point, I haven't gone back to it because I've been so afraid of feeling that I couldn't be a lesbian and still meditate.

Rose

I was a very religious Catholic, and I still am. The church never talked about homosexuality so my mind was very clear. I didn't grow up with hang-ups. Because nobody ever talked about it, I never thought about whether it was good or bad. When we lived in San Francisco and we started being around more and more gay people, that's when I found out the church's opinion. Other than that, I never knew. The only reason I found out was because people in San Francisco used to say, "Well, if the church finds out, I'm going to be excommunicated." I'd say, "That's a bunch of crap." The way I look at it, if you're comfortable with it, and it's actually love, not just a physical attraction, then there shouldn't be any question. Because God says, "Love each other." What you're loving is not the sex; you're loving the person. So there shouldn't be any question. So I never questioned.

The Pope himself just came out and said he would support homosexual people who couldn't be cured. In other words, if that was their lifestyle, what they actually wanted—they weren't just half and half and didn't know which one they wanted—he said for all the parishes to support them. That was about a year ago. It wasn't really good because of the way he said it: "If they are incurable." Everybody got uptight about it, but I thought it was neat. How often does anybody make any kind of stand like that? Even if they figure I'm incurable, well, that's all right. At least they accept me, you know? Really.

One time in Portland I went to my priest, and I said I wanted to talk to him about what he thought about gay people. He said, "Sure, come over." He didn't know I was gay.

So we talked to him, and he accepted it really pretty well. He said he hadn't met very many gay people that he knew of, who had come out to him, and he was quite ignorant on the subject. He said he'd like to learn some more about it. I said, "If you're going to kick me out of my church, it's too bad because it's not yours; it's mine. You can't do that. It's God's church; it's God's house." He says, "Well, I wouldn't. I would never kick anybody out of the church." I said, "It's too bad if you were going to because it's mine, not yours." They can't say whether you can go in or not.

It wasn't really that I was curious to see his reaction or because I was hung up about it or anything like that. At the time, there were some gay people having a hard time, not Catholics, just gay people here in our town. I thought if they could have somebody that they could talk to where they could feel comfortable, it would be really neat. And that's really mainly why I did it.

He said sure, he'd talk to any gay person who wanted to talk to him. I told him that if anybody did come, it wasn't because they wanted their minds changed, it was just because they wanted to talk to someone they could feel comfortable with. He said that would be great; he'd be more than happy to talk. I guess I didn't expect that response. I really didn't know what to expect because I'd never done anything like that before. It was a neat experience.

Jane Salter

I'm very traditionally Jewish. I've always been thrilled about Hanukkah, lit all the candles and said all the prayers. But I don't know that that connects me up religiously.

Judaism is very peculiar that way, because there are so many
cultural and traditional aspects that of course have religious
significance. But somehow in Judaism it's been all right to
do them your own way.

All religions are anti-gay. There's not a one of them that's
happy about having queers. But Judaism doesn't plague you
with sins. There is no heaven and hell; you rest in peace.
It's not set up so that you've got to answer to anybody: the
Church, the God, the Bishop, the Minister. You have to
answer to yourself.

Sally Gearhart told me that someplace in the Old Testa-
ment it says something directly negative about homosexuality, but I never heard anything about the subject when I
was growing up. They certainly didn't mention it in Sunday
school. You know, obviously, that it's not going to be cool
to say you're queer.

My parents certainly don't want my relatives in Nebraska
to know. In fact, when I was going to a Jewish lesbian group,
my mother freaked out. She said, "Jane, it's bad enough
lesbian, do you have to say Jewish lesbian?" She just doesn't
want us Jews identified that way. Jews are never queer; Jews
are never divorced; Jews are never unclean in any way. My
mother's an A-number-one Jewish chauvinist. All the bril-
liant people in the world have been Jewish, even if they said
they weren't.

I spend a lot of time with my relatives in San José, and
they know I'm gay. I would not feel comfortable if they did
not know. I just went to their house with a friend for
Hanukkah celebration, and my friend and I were very affectionate and open. At the end of the evening, we sat on the
couch together in each other's arms, and it was very comfortable.

I can't go into the synagogue and go to services now when
sometimes I'd like to because it is an extremely patriarchal

religion. In orthodox religions there are prayers that say, "Thank God I'm not a woman," and the women sit separate from the men.

On the other hand, the modern Jewish woman is a very strong woman, which is why I think so many lesbians are Jewish. There are oodles of Jewish lesbians. It's wonderful. I find that basically Jewish women are very strong. I feel good about that and proud behind that. There are lots of Jewish lesbians, and that just excites me no end.

I get a lot from my Judaism, from the closeness of Jewish people, and from the whole 5,740 years of collective consciousness which I feel. I feel like a Jew from back then until now. I feel rich in a lot of tradition that I can share with the women I love, and that's very important to me.

Dolores Rodriguez

I went to Catholic school for eight years. They tried to brainwash us so much that I just got turned off instead of turned on. I used to tell God in my own way, "I don't think I'm doing nothing wrong. I don't really feel it's wrong." That kept me from feeling guilty about the church.

One Christmas Eve, my grandmother, who's a very religious Catholic, came over and asked me to go to midnight mass with her. I put on this brown leather jacket, some beige slacks, and a sweater, and she looked at me and said, "¿Dónde está tu vestido?" ("Where is your dress?") I said, "Well, Grandma, I didn't bring one." She said, "Oh, but you can't go into the church with pants." I said, "Well, then I don't go to church." She said, "No, no, no. Come on."

She's known I was gay since I was real little. When I was seven or eight years old and I played with the little girl next door, she was the one who caught us and spanked my hands and said, "That's bad." She watched me very close after that, and she knew all along.

I walked with her to church that night. She wanted me to go to confession, so I went in, and I thought, "Well, you're here. Your grandmother's out there thinking you're really guilty; just tell the priest." So when he opened the little door, instead of saying, "Bless me, Father, for I have sinned," I just said, "Father, I'm here because my grandmother wants me to be here. I'm a lesbian, so she thinks I should be in here with you."

He said, "Ahem. Well, daughter . . ." And he told me it's fine to be a lesbian as long as it's real love, not a big sexual, flamboyant, flashing-light thing. If it's real and it's sincere and it's not full of all the garbage and the games, then it's okay.

So when I came out of confession, I was feeling really good, and I looked my grandmother right in the eyes and said, "Okay, I went to confession." I told her what the priest had said, and I said, "You're such a strong believer in the church, now you have to accept this." She said, "Okay, I guess that's all right."

Carol Gay

My religion wasn't real heavy. By the time I realized I was a lesbian, it had turned into a religion on the faith that things happen that are supposed to happen and everything will be okay. Nothing is judged in terms of right and wrong; it's just whatever is going on at the moment. Since my religion had already changed to that, I didn't have any religious problems.

Vera Freeman

I was a Methodist. I never felt like I was committing a sin by being gay. I felt like there was something wrong with me, but not that it was sinful. There was something wrong for me to feel that way because people kept saying you're not supposed to feel that way.

I got out of the church because I was kind of poor. We may have had a little money, but it was all going to support those kids and buy food. The church would make you feel small when you didn't give lots of money. So I decided that the church wasn't what I thought it was. It wasn't a refuge; it wasn't a place you could go to feel better. It was a place where they took money from poor people. What were they doing with that money? I didn't see anything they were doing with it. The church always looked the same; the pastor drove a Lincoln Continental. I didn't have anything, and I had to give ten dollars a week. It wasn't a matter of voluntary giving; it was a set fee.

Mary Howland

I come from a long family of ministers and missionaries. I went to four years of Bible college and studied for the ministry, but I realized near the end of it that while that was something I ought to do, it was not something I wanted to do. So I went into nursing.

In the thirteen years I was married, my husband, half out of belligerence and half out of plain good sense, didn't go along with a lot of my religious ways. So in that thirteen years, I mellowed down. When you're away from the emotionalism enough to get a good hard look at things, it is really helpful.

By the time of my divorce, I no longer considered myself even a practicer of the beliefs of that denomination. I knew—but wasn't able to prove by any doctrine—that whatever God there was, was the God who created whatever it was I was. And if that God created it, whatever I was, was okay. So I didn't have any religious problems.

Olivia Moreno

I was baptized a Catholic, but my father had his marriage to my mother annulled by the Pope so that he could marry my stepmother. So in the church's eyes, I can't be a Catholic because I am a bastard, illegitimate. But that's the religion I practiced more than anything else while growing up.

I really believe in God, and I'm very much a Christian. I see God as a gentle kind of God who's not going to condemn me because I love somebody. I've read books like *Lesbian Myth*, and I'm reading a book right now called *The Lord Is My Shepherd and He Knows I'm Gay*. It's saying that there's not a specific mention in the Bible about homosexuality that says it's wrong. I mean, it says it's wrong, but it also says it's wrong to eat meat on Fridays. There's so many things wrong, someone's going to do one of them all the time. I'm not going to be afraid that I'm going to burn in hell.

Theresa Reilly

I was raised in the Mormon church. When my high school lover died of a sudden illness, I had nobody to talk to and I was real crazy. I felt responsible for her death. God had taken her away so she wouldn't be perverted like me. It was a heavy time of guilt and pain.

After lots of searching within myself and going out with men, I finally met other lesbians at college, and I decided I was a lesbian and I could be proud and happy about it. Then I had another blow. My church found out about it and excommunicated me. I would be damned forever.

I had had no hint from the church that homosexuality was so awful. I hadn't come in contact with anybody who had been thrown out for being homosexual. I guess the church's stand on marriage and family should have been enough to clue me in. When you're resurrected and rise again to become gods and goddesses, you have to have been married in the temple. I hadn't really thought about that.

The church found out because I had given some lectures on homosexuality in a university psychology class. Someone in the class had been in my old church district, and he told my bishop I had said I was a homosexual. So my bishop called my mother to find out where I lived. My mother gave him my new address, and one of his counselors came up and served a summons on me, asking me to come talk to them at a bishop's court. He didn't say what it was about; he just said they wanted to talk to me.

So I went to talk to them, and they said they had information I was a lesbian. Didn't I know that that was one of the horrible sins of the world, almost as bad as adultery? What the bishop wanted me to do was write a letter of apology to the classes I had talked to. I should tell them I said some things I thought I believed, but I really didn't, and I was sorry I led them astray. I should also ostracize myself from all the gay people I knew, just totally ignore them if I was taking classes with them. I should cloister myself off and start reading church books again.

I held positions of responsibility in the church. My bishop was very concerned that I had been leading all the young girls astray. He was laying out all these gross implications. He said I could be a lesbian as long as I was not a practicing lesbian. If I was a lesbian in word only, lived by myself, had no lovers, then that was fine with the church.

I couldn't believe he was really saying those things. I was so angry and frustrated I said something like, "You ought to try it, you might like it. Go ahead and excommunicate me." There was no way I could change his mind and show him that what I was, was normal and acceptable.

That was in February, but they didn't formally excommunicate me until June. Some of the bishop's counselors came by my house a couple of times to see if they could talk to me. I also got a letter from the state president, asking me if I wanted to talk to him.

One of the things they *didn't* tell me was that I could come to a special meeting where I could face my accuser, the student who had said this stuff. I could face him and have a discussion. Some of the things he had told the bishop weren't true.

In May, my mother came and told me she was going to leave the church if I was excommunicated. She said she had decided that any church that was so narrow-minded it couldn't let a person be what they were was not the right church for her, which was real wonderful. My older sister is very heavily into the church. She has a couple of kids she's raising in the church, so when I was excommunicated that was hard for her to deal with, but she told me she still loved me.

In June, they held a bishop's court, formally excommunicated me, and sent me a letter of excommunication. I was real blown away that the religious aspect of my life, eighteen years of my life, was just null and void. I had to go through a period of working out the things I believed in, in the church, what I still felt was valid, what wasn't valid.

I would probably be allowed in the church, but I would no longer be a member of the church, and my baptism was void. If I wanted to become a member of the church again, I'd have to start at the beginning. I would not be able to take the sacrament.

I had to work out the guilt I would probably feel if I ever walked into a church again. I would feel guilty mainly because of all the people who would know why I was excommunicated if I ever walked into my home district. Everybody there would know. The state president's daughter got pregnant when she wasn't married. They didn't excommunicate her, but everybody knew what was happening. All these people were making snide remarks about her. I wasn't prepared just to sit in meek subservience.

The only thing I could do was say, "This is me. If you don't like me, then what can I do? I'm not going to change for you." I felt that if I had said, "Okay, I'll do what you ask me to do," I would be living in sin more that way than I am now. I would be denying who I am, and I would still be lost somewhere with all this heavy burden of guilt and craziness. Not being able to say, "This is who I am," is just abdicating to someone else's pleasures.

I grew up in Utah and majored in theater in college. I assume I've got a B.A. in theater. I took my final during all this crazy time of excommunication and left. I left Utah because I had come to San Francisco for a lesbian conference, and I'd met a lot of lesbians I wanted to get to know better. It seemed like the avenues for my sexuality were more open in San Francisco than they were in Utah, and I didn't feel like sticking around. So I came to San Francisco and got involved with a women's band, did equipment for a year, and then played guitar for a year. I'm twenty-four.

Elizabeth Reilly

How did you learn that your daughter is a lesbian?

I had suspected that she was, but she hadn't told me, "Yes,

I am." Then it got to be a religious thing. Bill, my husband,
had been raised in the Mormon church, and so had Theresa.
I had joined the Mormon church. One day, Bill came home
from the priesthood meeting and said, "They're going to
excommunicate Theresa." I about died. I said, "Why?" He
said, "Because she's homosexual."

I was so angry. I was supposed to teach Sunday school,
and I called and said, "No way will I be there. Just get somebody else." I talked to a counselor in the bishopry who was
a friend and said, "No way will I come. I've just heard
they're going to excommunicate Theresa."

In about five minutes, all the bishopry were at my house,
and here I was in my nightdress. I was in a state of shock be-
cause at that time the Mormon church was my whole world.
I asked them how they knew Theresa was a homosexual.
They said she had said she was, in a class at the university.
Some little creep had gone to the bishop and said, "Theresa
is a homosexual; she's got to be excommunicated." I said,
"That is absolutely no proof."

Then I got mad. I said, "Why wasn't I informed of this?"
The bishop looked down his rotten bloody little nose at me
and said, "It's none of your business. It's a priesthood business." I said, "Bullshit. Then no way do I want anything
more to do with your church." I have never been back, and
I never will. I felt like a second-class citizen for the first time
in my whole life, that, as her mother and the person closest
to her, I would not be allowed to know what they were doing
to her.

In a way, the bishop had lied to me. He had called me before the excommunication and said, "Where is Theresa living? I think she might be happier if her records were in her
new church district." I said, "Oh, yes, she probably would,"
and gave him her address. What he really wanted was to take
her this summons to appear in bishop's court.

Then I felt really, really bad that a church would excommunicate a person because she was homosexual. I mean, God created us. Why would He create somebody the way that they are and then say, "Well, too bad you're that way. I'm not going to have anything to do with you." That isn't the God that I love.

That was four years ago, and I can still bawl, thinking about it. It was such an emotional thing to find out this way. Theresa, I guess, had been trying to hide it from me because she didn't want me hurt. And yet, I would much rather have heard it from her. I knew she was going through a horrible time, but I didn't know what it was.

At the time, I didn't know where Theresa was living. I knew she was still in the city, or she would have let me know. Bill works on Sundays, so I called a friend of mine who is not a Mormon, told him what was happening, and said, "I've got to find Theresa." He said, "Come on, let's go. We'll spend the whole day finding her."

I didn't know a lot of her friends at the university. I just went to the first one I could think of. We went from that friend to another to another. We went to all these bars. "Do you know where Theresa is?" "No, I don't know her." We went to cafes where I thought she might be. "No, I don't know her." I didn't know whether they were hiding the fact, or whether they really didn't know. We finally found her, and I said, "Why didn't you tell me? I would have understood." But, of course, Theresa is a very tenderhearted person and didn't want to hurt me.

She was living in a horrible mental state, because she thought she had already been excommunicated and that we probably wouldn't want to have anything to do with her. But to me, Theresa is more important than anything. Most of all, I wanted to find her and tell her I loved her and reassure her that there was no difference in my feeling for her.

I find a terrific love between lesbian women. Sometimes when I'm at home, I think about her being a lesbian, and I

wonder if she's missing out. There should be a nice relationship between a man and a woman, and she's always loved
children. But when I'm here with Theresa and I meet her
friends, and I realize all the love that there is between them,
I think, "No way. She's not missing anything."

Therapy

When you are in therapy, the therapist's attitudes about lesbianism are very important, whether or not you are talking about a problem obviously related to your lesbianism.

Most of the women I interviewed either said they had never had therapy or didn't mention it at all. Carol Gay didn't talk about therapy, but she did say that when she first came to California, she joined a coming-out group because she still had unfinished feelings, even though she had come out in Alabama.

Rose said, "I've never had any therapy. I don't feel I need any. If I do, I give it to myself. I just talk to myself. It's true, I do."

In addition to the lesbians you have already met, a new woman, Lana, will share her experiences with two different therapists and Alcoholics Anonymous.

Laverne Jefferson

When I got out of jail, I had ten conditions of parole. One of them was if the parole officer said that I had to go to therapy, then I had to go to therapy. My p.o. told me I was crazy; I'd go in and dance on his desk because I didn't like him. So he goes, "Okay, you are going to therapy."

I told this one therapist that I was gay, and she goes, "Oh, honey, oh, no!" She would try to cure me, and I said, "Look, I don't want to be cured. It ain't no disease; it's what I want to do." She'd say things like, "It's not normal." I'd say, "What do you know about normal with the kind of life you lead? You tell me, is it normal for you to have all those kids you got without a daddy?" So she just shut up, and I said, "Recommend me to another therapist," and I got another one.

The next therapist I got was gay, so she was all right. One time she started talking about her lover. Her lover's name was Pat, so it was really confusing. I asked, "Is Pat a male or a female?" At that time, me and my lover were both in therapy, and so even though she was scared about her job, she said, "She's a female." Then we started talking about the gay bar, and she helped me a whole lot. We became best friends.

Maria Gonzales

Once I went to therapy. I was nineteen, and I was confused. The therapist told me there was nothing wrong in me identifying with being a lesbian, that it was a real healthy attitude. He was also gay, the psychiatrist. He said, "Your confusion comes out of the social pressure for you to

be with a man. It doesn't mean that you're wrong." So I
just started accepting that.

Chrystos

The year before I broke up with my lover, I was seeing a
straight woman therapist who was always telling me that I
ought to get out of the relationship because it was damaging
to me. That was very true, but I kept thinking she was trying to tell me not to be gay, so I stayed in the relationship.

I finally stopped therapy with her because it was an in-
credible block not to be able to talk to her about what was
going on, not to have her understand, for instance, what it
means when you begin to make love to another woman vs.
being made love to all the time. She just couldn't understand what I was talking about.

Vera Freeman

I was going to a shrink for a while to keep from killing
everyone who was fucking with me and not allowing me to
grow, treating me as if I wasn't an American. I was down on
the whole United States: Black, white, anything.

This was after I was divorced and also after I separated
from the woman I moved out here with, which was really a
hard thing to get over. We'd been together for five years. It
took me damned near two years to get accustomed to knowing it was over. I kind of thought it would last forever.

Anyway, when I went to the shrink, I had to take this little
test: Minnesota Multiphasic, or something. There was only
two questions about being gay: when you were this age, did
you hate your mother more and love your father more; and
then again in the back, they asked the question: did you love

your mother more and hate your father? I wrote, "What's this?"

I did get a very nice shrink. He was really supportive. He was for my admitting to myself that that's the way I was, and why should I change.

Mary Howland

My first relationship with a woman lasted only eight months. Then I got into some counseling for myself.

I went in for my intake interview, and the therapist happened to be a man. He said, "Why are you here?" I spent about five minutes saying that I was needing to get through a lot of the things that caused my problems with my relationships. I got all done with that, and he said, "That's all well and good, but that's pretty long-term stuff you're talking about. It's stuff that I'm sure you need to deal with, but why are you so sad today?"

I looked at him, and I thought, "It's now or never." I said, "I've just broken up with my lover." He said, "Well, you're so terribly sad about that and grieving so badly, I think let's deal with the here and now and work from there."

Being from the TA Gestalt school, he asked me to work through some stuff. I got three sentences into it, and I looked at him and said, "I want very much to do this, but I can't hide something and still work. I simply need to tell you my lover's name is Anita." He said, "Fine. Then you put Anita in that chair, and you talk with Anita." And that was it. There was no problem.

Here in Minneapolis and all over the United States, there are more and more people in nursing, counseling, social work, psychiatry, and psychology who are realizing that homosexuality is a human condition, a natural state of being.

Jacqueline Denton

I'm not in therapy, but I do go to three support groups for women. It was easy enough to talk to the support group Mandy is in. There are three lesbians in that group, and I got a great deal of support from them.

The second support group I'm in is women around thirty. I was a little slower about telling them but knew I would have to, because of the intimate way we were all talking. I got a little uneasiness from two of the people in that group, but the others were very supportive.

In the older women's group, I really waited awhile, partly because we weren't meeting so regularly during the summer. When I did talk with them about it, I felt some real support from at least two of them. If some of them are uneasy, this is a matter for them to handle. It will definitely come up in the group again during the fall, because I will be talking about Sandra.

Tonya Holloway

It's been about a year since I realized that the label "lesbian" applied to me. I was in therapy with a man who really messed me over. I'd already had sexual relationships with women, and I popped out with, "You know, I think I'm a lesbian." He said, "Well, don't worry, I'll cure you." I said, "I really enjoy my relationships with women, and I don't think I want to be cured by you. I'm not happy with myself, with my life, but I am happy with the woman friends I know, and I don't want that taken care of."

It had taken me a long time to get to the point of telling him, and he came up with that "cure you" bit. The next time

I went to see him, he kept mentioning cases of his: "This person thought he was homosexual, but now he's got a nice relationship with his wife." I said, "Well, that's nice for him."

Every time he'd talk about homosexuals, he'd say how much he cured them, how well he brought them back into the world as normal people. After that time, I just walked out of the office and never went back. It wasn't worth my while to fight him on that. There were more things wrong with me at the time than that.

After I left him, it took me about seven months, and then I started going to a feminist therapist. I told her, "I think I'm a lesbian." She said, "Okay." That was that. I went to her for ten weeks, and it was so nice. She supported me through a lot. I took massive steps with her. All I needed was somebody to stand behind me and say, "Go ahead. You can do it if you want to."

Lana M.

I'm an alcoholic. Almost six years ago I stopped drinking and joined Alcoholics Anonymous. A.A. has done so much for me; I can't talk about myself without talking about it.

I think I numbed my feelings for women by drinking. All of my sexual experiences were when I was drunk—with men and with women, too. So when I stopped drinking, everything opened up and just seemed to come alive.

At the beginning of the time I went to A.A., I was in the closet, including to myself. I was in a women's group, and a number of the women turned out to be lesbians. Later, we formed a lesbian group of about a hundred alcoholic lesbians, but even in the other A.A. groups, I knew that to get help I would have to talk about being a lesbian, and so I did. It was very accepted. It's a very accepting group of people.

For a while, I was also in a therapy group. When I took to

the group the fact that I'd slept with a woman and that I was troubled by it, the leader said, "What troubles you about it?" I said, "I guess it's because I'm afraid people won't like me."

He said, "Who are you worried more about being bothered by this, the men or the women?" I said, "The women." He said, "Do you want to go around the room and see how people feel about it?" So I went around the room. Some people thought it was interesting, one of the women was kind of scared, but everyone was very supportive. I was lucky.

For five years previous to this, I had been with another therapist, Dr. Johnson. During this time, I went through an experience with a woman where I was crawling in bed with her and cuddling. I felt sexual feelings that I wasn't calling sexual, and I really liked it, but I couldn't see anywhere to go from there, and neither could she.

I told my experiences to Dr. Johnson, and he just put it down. He said, "Oh, it's just wanting to be warm." Each time I brought it up, that was his response. When I suggested that maybe I was a lesbian, he said, "Homosexual relationships are frustrating."

He was into a deadpan psychologist thing. He never showed any emotions at all. He rarely gave any advice, but this was one of the issues on which he did give advice, "If you're not a lesbian, don't go around sleeping with women. You just want the warmth, and it's frustrating." I guess it would have been frustrating if I ended up just cuddling without having any sexual experiences!

I also told Dr. Johnson that I had always wanted to turn into a boy. I had an older brother, and he had all the privileges, was able to do things I wasn't able to do, and was excused for things I wasn't excused for. So I expected to turn into a boy when I was ten years old. I even had my name picked out. Dr. Johnson just laughed.

In A.A., we have these suggested steps to recovery, and one of them is to clear up the past. Interpreting that broadly, I wanted to straighten out Dr. Johnson. So I went to him and told him about alcoholism—since he hadn't understood the disease of alcoholism, either—and I told him about lesbianism. I told him how wonderful it is to be a lesbian and to feel this way.

His response was, "Um hm. Um hm." He asked a few questions like, "Do you think your alcoholism is related to your lesbianism?" I said, "Of course not. Alcoholism is a disease, and lesbianism is just a direction, a series of feelings that I have. They're independent."

I'm fifty years old. I grew up on an orange grove in southern California and at age ten moved to Los Angeles. I went to college in premed but ended up in research. After school, I moved from L.A. to Chicago to New York to Paris, always looking for the promised land. It was in Paris that I started drinking in an alcoholic way. I've been working in New York, but now I'm planning to go live in the country with other dykes.

Out in the World

Discrimination

One of the most common anxieties a woman who has just realized she is a lesbian has to face is, "What's out there in the way of discrimination or harassment, and how will I deal with it?" In earlier chapters the lesbians described how they reacted to blatant or subtle harassment in relation to children, school and work, religion, etc. Here they specifically address the issue of discrimination itself.

Rose said she hadn't ever experienced discrimination that she knew of, and Jackie said, "I'm impossible. I wouldn't notice discrimination if it was around." The rest of the lesbians, however, have noticed and dealt with discrimination in their lives.

Carol Queen

I think any gay person who has spoken on panels, or walked down the street hand in hand with a lover, experiences ripples of discomfort from some people and great waves of disapproval from other people, if I may use a little oceanic metaphor. I've experienced both, and I am bothered by it. I can cope with somebody's disapproval perfectly adequately, but if somebody should be schizo and disapproving enough to want to do something to me, then there's not a whole lot I could do to fight it. If somebody wants to put a brick through my window, my window is gone. If somebody wants to accost me in an alley, then I'm gone. I try not to be paranoid, but just because I'm not paranoid doesn't mean they're not out there.

Eugene is a bad place to be for that kind of thing. It's a good place to be for being gay, because it's still small and warm and community-oriented, but it's in the middle of Oregon, which is an essentially conservative agricultural and foot-stompin' logger state.

In the last six to eight months [1976], Eugene has really been hit by harassment. A women's bookstore got its window smashed twice by rocks with nasty notes attached. Somebody also wrote nasty things on the bookstore door in felt pen.

On Stonewall Day, the gay people of Eugene had a rally and march and gathering in the park. It was really very sizable, with television coverage and banners and chants. We went past the Olympic trials, chanting "Two, four, six, eight, Olympic athletes aren't all straight." A couple of them obviously weren't; they gave us very big grins when we went by. Anyway, it was a much bigger show of gay solidarity than Eugene had ever seen. The day after all that, the storefront window of Starflower was smashed. Starflower is a primarily lesbian-owned natural foods distributing company. Somebody also took a chunk of concrete and smashed the windshields of Starflower's trucks. There was a nasty note involved in that one, too.

Eugene has one gay bar. It's downtown. Most people know that it's primarily a gay bar. It's not a very nice bar, but

then, you take what you can get, right? There's a guy who
works in the parking structure just a little ways down the
street from the bar. He's got to be the most notorious homo-
phobe in Eugene. On infrequent occasions, rains of eggs
have been known to shower down from the overpark on
passing couples. It's a real weird coincidence that the couples
almost always happen to be gay.

Somebody threw a chunk of liver into the bar, and somebody left a dead animal on the doorstep one night. Then
they got a little bit heavier and splashed some acid-base,
impossible-to-get-off paint on the door of the bar, on some
of the patrons' cars, and on the owner's car. One of the own-
ers is a big straight business person around here, and he
didn't like that a bit.

There's an organization out at a local community college
which is called Student Organization to Eliminate Queers.
It's not an up-front organization; we've only heard of it once,
but once was enough. One day somebody found a mimeo-
graphed invitation to a meeting of the Student Organization
to Eliminate Queers. The meeting time and place just happened to be the same as that of the Gay People's Alliance
meeting that night. Fortunately, nobody came into the GPA
meeting. All they did was send a shower of rocks and a
couple of beer bottles over the fence, but that kind of thing
makes a person real paranoid.

We think the SOEQ is run by the same dude in the parking structure. He has a personal vendetta against a very
nice, young, gay broadcasting student. He splashed this
student's van with the same acid-base paint, wrote "Queer"
on the side very big, smashed the windshield, then called in
a death threat to the radio station at midnight.

When my picture was in the paper two weeks ago, my
mother received an obscene call, because I didn't have a
phone at that point. (Actually, there are three or four
Queens in the phone book, and I wonder if some totally

unrelated person didn't get a weird call first.) Occasionally, I get quite frightened. I think there are probably some sickies out there, and I hope I don't ever run into one of them.

At the same time, I can see a lot of concrete and positive change associated with my being out and open and talking to groups. We did a lovely panel for an adult education class up in Albany, which is a very small, provincial place. It was mainly older people, and we talked to them for three hours. They were very open and asked wonderful questions. Here were people our parents' age or a little younger, and we didn't think they would react favorably at all. They had written down questions for us to answer in case they were too defensive to ask questions out loud. We got the first one off the paper, and after that it was just spontaneous.

So with that kind of thing, I can see change happening. I can see it happening every time an uptight, defensive gay person comes to Gay Youth and two meetings later they're mouthing off with everybody else. That kind of stuff really makes it worthwhile. So let them come with their bricks. I'll get new windows, what the hell.

Laverne Jefferson

One Halloween, I was visiting a lady in San Francisco. We were on a bus, and another gay couple was on the bus, too. We were sitting in back rapping, and the other two were up in front kissing and stuff, just being themselves. You know, San Francisco, anything goes. This one guy got on the bus, sat down, and saw these two ladies kissing. So the next stop he got off the bus and started yelling, "You fucking queers, you fucking lesbians!" We all jumped up and said, "Get your fucking ass back on the bus, you little chump." He just stood out there, screaming and screaming.

That's the only time anything like that ever happened to me. It didn't really happen to me because I wasn't kissing, but it was the same thing; he just didn't know it.

Jeri

I've never experienced discrimination in any form, and I don't know why not. I was working on discrimination surveys for the Portland Town Council, and I was amazed at the number of gay people who have been discriminated against. The discrimination is used in its most vicious form. It's very subtle, the kind you can't put a finger on. While I knew it existed, I didn't know the extent of it.

Maria Gonzales

I feel discrimination all the time. I don't know how I handle it. I just let it slide, I guess.

You tell a straight man that you're a lesbian, and the whole attitude is this conquest trip. "Well, you haven't fucked the right man yet." I say, "No, I haven't and I don't need to."

I used to get this thing from lesbians, "You should try a man sometime, because unless you know what the other side is like, you can't really appreciate a woman." That is total bullshit to me. Shit, I don't need to find out what a man is like, I *know* what a woman is like. That's all I need to know. In that sense, I've felt discriminated against.

Chrystos

In the last three years since I've been really out as a dyke to the world with no going back, I've gotten to a place where

I don't put myself in situations where I'm going to have to face discrimination. I'm very careful to arrange my life so that nothing gets to me.

I know there is a lot that is closed to me because of being gay. For instance, I write poetry, and I'm clear that there aren't very many places for my poetry to go because it is dyke poetry. Not that I always write about being a dyke, but my stance is different. So there's discrimination in the sense that I wouldn't be acceptable to the majority of the poetry publishers.

The last place I lived I eventually had to leave because I was a dyke. The woman managing the place made it very uncomfortable, and I know that had to do with the fact that I was a dyke. She was real uptight about it. I think it would be very difficult to find a place to live as an out-and-out dyke.

Most of the kinds of discrimination I feel a lesbian suffers are not up-front and verbal. It's not something like racism that people feel more comfortable in being obvious about. Being a lesbian is something dirty. Most people don't even want to acknowledge it enough to say, "You're a queer." They'd much rather just be cold or give you a hard time.

I'm very conscious of the kind of vibrations that come in at me when I'm walking down the street with a woman. Most of the time I'm ready to get in a fight if I have to. I don't have a car, so I take the bus a lot. I'm constantly aware of the danger it is to be a dyke out on the streets late at night. So far, I've only been in three fights about it.

One of them was at the corner diner. I was waiting for the bus, and this guy came up to me and said something about queer. First I just ignored him, but he wouldn't leave me alone, so I turned around and punched him in the stomach. I'm pretty sure he had been drinking, and he was really surprised. I don't feel comfortable fighting with men unless I take them by surprise, because I know I'm not that strong and I don't want to get creamed. I had seen that the bus was almost across the street, so I figured I would punch him and then by the time he got up again I'd get on the bus and take off, which is exactly what I did. It wasn't really a fair fight, but I don't feel as though, as a lesbian, I can fight fairly. I have to get my licks in when I can.

Another one was when I was coming home pretty late one night. I was walking, and some guys with knives surrounded me. I wasn't too sure what they wanted, whether it was money or rape or just to hassle me. I started sweet-talking them because I realized there was not very much I could do. Then, when there was a space in their ranks, I just took off running. I think when you do something that surprises someone like that, it takes them a minute to figure out what's going on, and then they let it go. They just want somebody who will stand still and let them do whatever they're going to do. They don't want to have to run and get all hepped up.

The third fight was when I was with another woman. We started getting hassled by some guys, and we just kept walking really fast. Eventually, one of them came up and started to say something to the other woman who was very butchy-looking. She just punched him real fast right at the breastbone, which is a good place to hit because it knocks the wind out of somebody. He went down, and the rest of them just left.

Those weren't real fights; they were more like confrontations I managed to escape from without great bodily damage. But since that time, I never walk anywhere. I ride my bicycle, and I keep my dog with me. I haven't had any trouble since I do that. She's a friendly dog, but she's big, and a lot of people are afraid of dogs, so that seems to do the trick. Also, when you're on a bicycle and you're moving, it's very difficult for someone to hassle you. I always cross the street if I see a big group of kids.

Esther Brown

I have never admitted to any of the straight community here that I'm a lesbian. It's a small community, and I have a paper route. I used to be quite active in the Grange and that sort of thing, and you still can't just say, "I am."

When I'm out in public, I conduct myself in an acceptable manner for the public. I have gone to the extent of having an all-woman ranch, which I'm sure is a great topic of conversation in the neighborhood. Although the neighbors don't condone it, I guess they must be accepting it because they still speak to me, and they've been very helpful any time I've really had an emergency. When I dumped the Caterpillar tractor in the creek, all the neighbors came over and winched it out. One of the neighbors took care of me for a week after I wrenched my back, when I couldn't get in and out of the tub or bed or anything else. These are straight people.

Canyon Sam

I'm always going to be in places that are fairly safe for lesbians to be in, which means I'm limited in where I can go in the world. But I've got to take care of myself in that way. I would never go to Texas and be a heavy-duty dyke. I would get stabbed in the back by red-necks. I could go to places where it's not safe to be out as a lesbian, but I'd have to avoid making myself overtly conspicuous, so that men wouldn't get threatened and take me off somewhere.

Jane Salter

Because I'm blind, people are very intimidated, and, of course, I walk arm in arm with any companion. I get away with all kinds of shit, and I'm excused because I'm blind.

I used to speak in colleges about being blind. If the subject of lesbianism would come up, everything would change. Everything I'd said about being blind was invalidated, and suddenly all they heard was that I was queer. For instance, the first time I spoke, one woman said, "Did losing your sight affect your relationships?" I was evasive, and I said, "I'm having a very nice relationship." She said, "How does he relate to this?" It was the very first time I was speaking. I had a minute's panic, and then I said, "It's not he; it's she, and she does have some problems around it. Some of her friends think she's really great for relating to a blind woman. But you know what? That's her problem." And then I went on. There was dead silence in what had been a very talkative classroom. It was really heavy.

I was hospitalized for the first time last December because of my diabetes, and I was almost dead when I got there. They put me in a private room because I was screaming and hollering so much. They wanted to put me in intensive care, and I said I wouldn't go. This friend of mine convinced the doctor that she would take care of me all night, but the nurses didn't get the order. They came to wheel me to intensive care, and these six dykes stood around my bed and said, "Sorry, she's not going anywhere." And I didn't.

We had General Hospital upside down. The hospital couldn't get me the kind of food they wanted me to eat, so my friends cooked everything and brought it in for ten days. This little room was constantly jammed with people. Eventually, people took to sleeping with me in bed there. At first the staff was hysterical about it all, but their attitudes changed a lot.

One friend, Susan, had been there often. Before I left, another friend was sleeping with me, and this nurse walked in. She looked at us, started to walk out, looked at us again and said, "Where's Susan?" Then she caught herself and said, "Well, I just wanted to see who was sleeping with you tonight."

I went to another hospital in April where we did our number there, and to Presbyterian Hospital in November. The whole first night I was at Presbyterian I was hysterical, sobbing wildly, and my friend stayed there in bed with me all night, holding onto me. The staff didn't like it, but it was too bad. I wouldn't stay in the hospital without somebody.

A lot of the doctors at Presbyterian were gay, and we related to them real well. As a matter of fact, I liked the way the staff related to me and the other women as a total. They didn't treat us like we were invisible or freaks.

My doctor at the General Hospital diabetes clinic said she thought my lesbian lifestyle was really supportive to my health. I have to go to the hospital once a month for tests. My women friends always come with me and take care of me, and we're a force together.

Dolores Rodriguez

I've been lucky. I found a gay job, and I got involved with Gay Latinos. (GALA). Los Angeles is such a freaky place; there's so many gays running around that there's hardly any discrimination here. But that's why I'm here. I don't think I could survive someplace else because of all the discrimination against gay people.

It's especially hard if you look gay, if you have fallen into that damn role trip. I have an older friend who's Filipino; she's forty-six or so, and she looks like a dyke. She still can't find a job, and she's gone through job-training programs. She refuses to change the way she dresses because she's always dressed that way since she was a teenager.

A cop harassed me one time in Sacramento. He came to

the car window, and he knew I was a woman by my license, but he kept calling me sir, just to bug me. "Oh, excuse me, *Ma'am.*" He had that sarcastic look on his face and tone in his voice. Then he went back to the police car to write the ticket, and him and his partner were laughing away in the car.

When I was in Sacramento, people wouldn't rent to me and my lover. They'd look at her and they'd look at me and say, "Nope." It was always rented out or somebody had just walked away with the key—all that bullshit.

In Sacramento, I lived in the Chicano district. When I was walking down the street, low-riders would come by and yell, "Queer, dyke!" Sometimes they'd stop the car, and I'd take off the other way.

Carol Gay

I've lived in a fantasy world ever since I've labeled myself lesbian. I was either hanging out with this real nurturing, cohesive group at the bar in Mobile, or in the fantasy world of San Francisco where you can be a dyke among one thousand other dykes.

In Mobile, dykes are invisible in some ways. Ninety percent of the people there don't know what a lesbian is and wouldn't know one if they saw one. So there's no one for them to discriminate against, because they think lesbians are not there.

Here in the Bay Area, we've got our own community, and you can function just within that community. You can take classes in the community; you can get your car worked on by lesbians only; you can get carpentry done by lesbians only; you can go to lesbian doctors; you can go to lesbian therapists. Your whole world can be this lesbian fantasy world, so it's been hard to notice any discrimination.

Vera Freeman

I can't say that I ever really worried about discrimination. At one time, I did want to tell the world I was gay, but I decided that it wouldn't be cool. I looked around at people; they're all a bunch of conservative red-necks, and you just don't tell them. You don't talk to them, because they're sitting there waiting to get some dirt on you.

Mary Howland

I have a feeling that some of the trash that gets thrown into the backyard and the abuse of our dogs last summer was by the teenagers who sort of put two and two together. It wasn't happening to anyone else. All the adults in the neighborhood like us, though, and I'm sure they know. Not that we've done anything in front of the windows, or anything. We've never shared anything about our gay activities with them; we just act like they already know it. We go over and have a beer with them and talk about the weather or the new shrubs we planted. We don't sit around holding hands, but neighbors don't sit around holding hands. It's just not necessary.

Most of the discrimination I've experienced has been within the gay community. Both Lisa and I are well known and well liked, but other gay people find us threatening because we're open. We're open about our love for each other, and we do public speaking. Lisa's been on television and in the newspapers two or three times, and we produced a film on lesbians for Channel 10. We have lost several friends who still love us and phone us but who won't come see us and who won't be seen with us, because if they're seen with us somebody might think they're gay. Some of them have actually had to cut off all contacts with us.

A lot of the strange discrimination we get from the gay community is because of the kind of people we are. We're both open, positive people, and our lives are just as open and constructive and stable as if we were straight. And why not? Most gay people are that way. We don't look over our shoulders all the time, and we don't worry if somebody puts two and two together. People get to know us for who we are, and then when they find out we're gay, sometimes it blows their minds.

Olivia Moreno

I speak on panels sometimes for the Gay People's Alliance. I'll be walking down the street with another woman, and someone who has seen the panel will see us and say, "Faggot," or something like that, but it doesn't bother us.

The person I'm involved with right now is really in the closet because she's in an occupational situation where she has to be. She's a graduate student at the college in a fairly conservative department. It's really hard when I see her on campus, and I can't go up and hug her and say, "Have you had a good day?"

Politics and the Law

If you are a lesbian, your rights to employment and housing are generally not protected, and in many states what you do in bed is illegal. Society's laws and attitudes concerning lesbianism may indeed affect your political views, as some women in this chapter point out.

Carol Queen is not included, because she talked about her politics in the realization section. Mary Howland, while not specifically discussing any changes in her political perspective, has been very active in gay rights activities: speaking, leading workshops, helping produce a film. Maria, Canyon, and Jane didn't address this issue.

Laverne Jefferson

My politics didn't change at all. I'm not into system politics, anyway. I've got my own politics—it's called learn-

ing to survive in society. That's my politics. Being gay is not
going to change that at all, because I'm going to do what I
have to do to survive and to have my son survive. I'm not
into politics because it don't do anything for me. It just
keeps me poor.

Jeri

It never bothered me that it was against the law. I always
thought it was a joke that they would try to regulate what
people did in their own bedrooms. And I've never had any
fears of police busting in my house at night. I remember
having a big celebration New Year's Eve going into '72 here
in Oregon, because we were finally legal, but that's the one
time I ever paid any attention to it.

I'm a very political person. In 1964, I worked on Gold-
water's campaign, identified myself as a Conservative, and
belonged to Young Americans for Freedom, which is a very
conservative, John Birch-type youth group. It wasn't until
the McGovern campaign that anybody talked much about
gay rights on either side, so I stayed in the Conservative
party for a long time. Well, in '72 it started looking a little
more favorable to take a stand, so I had something to go by.

Today I identify myself as a liberal Democrat. I've pretty
well come full circle, as far as my political identification,
and I would say that almost 90 percent of that is due to the
gay rights aspect.

The gay rights issue in the political parties has changed
my thinking on lots of other things, too. I find my ideas on
nuclear power, welfare spending, defense, all those things
are different from what they might have been had I not been
involved in gay rights.

One time, I came out to a politician who was campaigning
for state representative. He was a guy I had gone to Sunday

school with when I was a little kid. He came to the house
and said, "Hi. I'm running for state representative. Do you
have any questions you want to ask me?" Unbeknownst to
Rose, he had already responded to the gay rights question-
naire. So I knew how he stood on it, but she didn't. She said,
"How do you stand on gay rights?" He said, "Ah, er, well,
I think gay people ought to have their rights."

I was in the kitchen at the time. I came walking out and
said, "Hi. I bet you don't remember me." He looked at me
and got this panicky, blank look on his face. "No, I don't."
I said, "Well, I'm Jeri. I used to go to Sunday school with
you." He said, "Well, what do you know? Gee, you've
changed a little bit." I said, "Yeah, so have you. One of the
reasons Rose is asking that is because we're gay, and we're
very interested in knowing how you stand on gay rights. It
makes a difference on how we're going to vote."

When I said those words to him, I knew he had the same
religious background I did, and I knew he was a politician
who's not always going to say what he thinks but what he
thinks is right politically. We had a really neat conversation,
and now he's bragging to all the politicians about this really
good friend of his who's gay.

Chrystos

My politics have really changed since I've been out as a
lesbian. I was sort of a George McGovern-liberal person. I
don't feel like I'm very radical now, in the sense that I'm not
storing bombs away in my basement for the revolution. But
I feel as though the things that I'm doing in my life are
radical changes. I give a lot of energy to a women's coffeehouse, and to me that's a political statement: women are important enough to give a lot of my energy to, rather than
giving it to McGovern or some abstract person.

So my sense of what politics are has really changed. I don't pay much attention to what's going on in the hierarchy, because it doesn't apply to me anymore. I don't identify with it. What is political to me is what happens on the streets, how I interact with other women in a collective, what kind of support I give to other women, how tolerant and flexible I'm able to be in the community so that I'm not judging people. Politics for me are very personal now.

As far as the law goes, I have a lot of paranoia. It's not specifically illegal anymore in California for consenting adults to do whatever they want behind closed doors, but I have a whole sense of the fact that it's going to be an extremely difficult fight to make lesbianism legal and a fact of life throughout the world. I feel like we won't be safe in any sense until that happens in an irreversible way, and I don't know if that will happen in my lifetime. I'm very conscious of the fact that if the government decides to get uptight, that's the end of all of us.

Esther Brown

It wasn't until I moved here to Washington that I became interested in politics at all. I sat in on one meeting where the Women's Commission was preparing the format of its proposal to the city council and the mayor. Other than that, I haven't really been too involved in politics or the Women's Movement.

Through the woman I was living with, I've become a little more aware of these things. In her past, she has been quite active and expressive in her attitudes about lesbian women and their place in society. She's twenty-one and has just graduated from the university here. Her attitudes have rubbed off on me somewhat.

She hasn't changed me to the degree where I would go

up to a stranger and say, "Are you a lesbian?" I'm still conservative to that point. However, she would not be reluctant to do it. I think the trend currently is more—why beat about the bush, why be a closet case? Once you've made that decision, give it your all.

I would never go on a panel and say, "I am, and I think everyone else should be." Unfortunately, many women today have that tendency. They think it's so great that that's the only way for anyone, and I don't go along with that. I figure each individual as a woman should be able to decide for herself in her own time. Sometimes it takes years and years and years. In the current generation, it might happen within a short time of getting out of school, or while in college. They can admit it because women are becoming stronger. They have support, which we didn't have.

Rose

I still consider myself conservative. I'm really kind of a radical conservative. I think they should get a few things straightened out. Our law should be passed; we should have our rights.

In a way, being gay made me a little more aware, and it made me get a little more involved in politics than I probably would have before, but that's about it.

Dolores Rodriguez

I've been political since high school. I started getting involved with United Farmworkers in eleventh grade, and then I helped get the Chicano studies and the Black studies going in my high school.

In junior college, I was really involved with MECHA

(Mexican American Students and Latin American Studies),
but to me MECHA was just like a little social clique. You
were all working together, but you were also screwing each
other and partying with each other, and I didn't want to
do it with any of them. So I ran into problems there.

One reason I moved to Los Angeles was because it is so
political. Right now, I'm working on organizing some Latina
women, especially those who are coming out and have been
through bad experiences. I'm also working with GALA (Gay
Latinos).

I've seen a lot of my friends screwed over on dope and
not getting out of a pit. You can get so stuck into it. I said,
"I might be a dyke, but I'm not staying in no pit. I'm going
out there and try to do something about it."

Carol Gay

I didn't have any politics when I first came out. There I
was in Alabama, and politics was Jimmy Carter raising pea-
nuts on his farm. That was politics. There were no women's
politics.

Just within the last few years could you start getting *Ms.*
magazine in Mobile, and there are no lesbian magazines
down there at all. I went to the bookstore once to order
Patience and Sarah, a lesbian novel, and they wouldn't even
order it for me. So I had no exposure whatsoever to lesbian
politics because I'd never gotten a publication, a book,
anything.

When I got to San Francisco, I was suddenly inundated
with politics. At first I was real angry because I thought
women were being too heavy on one another. I still think it
gets a little overly political here, but I needed to learn a
lot of the politics because I'd just never been exposed to
them. So changing my politics was real heavy for me.

Illegality doesn't mean much to me. I don't ever think of it as, "Oh, it's against a law. I could be put in prison." I just don't think about things like that. I've been arrested for dope smoking before, and that to me was just a farce, just real funny.

Vera Freeman

I thought about it being illegal, but I didn't worry about it, no. I didn't worry about it because there are too many of us. Why would they single me out? As long as I didn't demonstrate in front of my neighbors or do a public thing, why should I be arrested?

It's not illegal here in Oregon. In Michigan it's illegal, but there are millions of gay people there, too. That's where I grew up, and that's where I learned everything.

Olivia Moreno

It really hasn't affected my politics that much. I'm pretty conservative in all other aspects of my life, besides being gay. Like I don't think people should insult the Pope. I used to be a Republican, I think, but I'm a Democrat now, basically because they're supposed to be for the people.

I'm still a capitalist. All my friends freak out and say, "How can you be gay and be a capitalist at the same time?" But I just am. I'll probably be a capitalist until I die; being gay doesn't have anything to do with that. The person I'm involved with right now is a socialist. She calls me a capitalist pig, and I call her a socialist pig.

As far as the law goes, I can do anything I want to with someone over eighteen as long as they're consenting. Washington's a pretty good state, except that it's not against the law to discriminate. If our landlady knew that I was gay she would probably kick us out, and she would have every legal right to do so. Unfortunately.

My first lover was sixteen, but it didn't really bother us because I was under eighteen, too, so there was not much anybody could do about it. Her parents couldn't prosecute me because I was underage, and it would mean that she was involved with me. My parents couldn't prosecute her because she was underage. So there was nothing anybody could have done except put us both in jail, and as long as we were together, we probably wouldn't have cared. Now, since I have turned eighteen, I haven't been involved with anybody under eighteen. I won't. It's too much of a risk.

Jacqueline Denton

My politics are getting much more radical as a direct result of being much more aware of what lesbians are up against. For instance, there was a lesbian mothers' conference not too far from New York. Sandra, not having any children, volunteered to do the child care for the mothers and asked me to go, too, and help her with it. I felt really good about that. I have a feeling I could get myself involved in doing some work for the lesbian mothers, or something like that.

I hadn't really been political before. I mean, I talked political, and I once knew how to write a letter to the authorities and make noise. I gave some money to groups, but that was about it.

Lana M.

I'm an anarchist, and I just don't believe in most of their laws. So many of their laws are just ways of controlling people. I can't accept that anyone can legislate my right to love a woman, to have sex with a woman. That's unthinkable. I don't accept that law.

Before I came out as a lesbian, I was into pretty radical politics as a radical pacifist. I'd committed acts of civil disobedience and gotten busted for sitting in for pacifist things. I think I had found a lot of my identity by identifying with oppressed groups. I must have felt oppressed internally, so it was easy to march for civil rights or the political prisoners in Vietnam.

In fact, the first time I called myself a lesbian was at a political rally. There was a gay rights bill at the City Council of New York. My lover was very political and was going to be at the rally outside of City Hall while they were debating the bill inside. I'd marched for years as a radical pacifist, but I found myself hedging on whether to go out. It's only later I've realized how much I was hedging because there were going to be television cameras there. Even though my lover was a woman, I had never called myself a lesbian. In fact, I was even still imagining I would look around for a man sometime.

But I went out there, and it was raining. It was awful. I found myself getting caught up in identifying with the people who were there. I was surrounded by men and women who had been really damaged by the attitudes of the public and by the legislation. There were people who had actually lost their jobs because they had come out. They had put a lot of energy into trying to get the bill passed, talking to the public, talking to council people. They were just standing there in the rain.

There was a lot of love and a lot of hope. But it wasn't passed, and there was a lot of anger and a lot of tears. Even though I hadn't been a part of the struggle, it really touched me.

After that vigil, I called myself a lesbian, and I said it

proudly. That was five years ago when I was forty-five.

Since coming out, I've been moving away from politics and getting more interested in my inner life. I don't have to identify with other oppressed people anymore, and I don't have to be oppressed internally anymore. The impulses that allowed me to recognize myself as a lesbian, to love myself as a lesbian, are the things that meant I didn't have to march anymore.

I guess I also think marching is kind of futile. We can't change anyone but ourselves. We can only do whatever we can do by our own vibrations, our own radiations to the people around us. We can change others by just being happy.

I guess whatever you do in your life is politics, though. I'm a separatist now, in the sense that I relate only to women. I'm also writing a book that's political, in that it has to do with the institutions of the patriarchy that I hate. You see, I think of politics as being a very male thing, and I want us to find new alternatives to everything, so I don't even use the word politics anymore.

Culture

Women who belong to cultural minorities not only have to deal with the surrounding white society's attitudes toward lesbians, but with the attitudes of their own culture as well. How do their ethnic groups feel about lesbians? How does the lesbian subculture feel about them as ethnic minorities? How do they deal with the triple oppression of being a woman, a lesbian, and an ethnic minority?

A new woman, Ana Torres, adds a unique perspective as she discusses her feelings about "coming out" as a Chicana, as well as a lesbian.

Laverne Jefferson

I was living in this town with a lady for six years, and it was just full of Black people that I knew. They never saw me out with the guys anymore, and they all put it together.

I started dealing marijuana and drugs out of my house, so

they would come over. All that would be at my house was a
bunch of ladies: short hair, long hair, kissing and hugging.
If they had come up to me and asked me if I was gay, I'd
have said, "Yeah," and that would have been that. But they
didn't. They just figured that's how it was, and they respected me for it.

Now they say, "I know Laverne. She used to live with this
Irish girl." "Yeah, the girl that all the niggers been after.
Laverne must got something, because that Irish girl just
wouldn't leave her." They don't mess with me because I've
known them for a long time.

Maria Gonzales

Right after high school I went to Puerto Rico, and in
Puerto Rico, of course, it's fine to be butch, because among
the gay people there, that's all there is: butch and femme.
At that time I wasn't political, in the sense of feminism. I
didn't know what feminism was. I just knew what I was and
who I was.

I knew what I had been dealing with as a woman growing
up, and yet when I came back to the States, I had women
come up to me because I'm butch and say, "You don't know
what it's like being oppressed sexually all your life." I said,
"Are you kidding? What are you talking about? I know what
sexual oppression is. I think my culture invented sexual
oppression."

I resent being called macho if I'm acting butch. If you're
gay and Third World, you're really heavy butch, and if you
come on really heavy butch, you're really macho. Nobody's
got the right to tell me I'm being macho. I got the right to tell
myself, and maybe another Latina has the right to tell me,
but I get really offended when a white woman tells me I'm
being macho. That trip's been laid on me all my life. I don't

even need to hear it. I know what macho is, and I've never been a macho. Well, when I was growing up, I was a little macho. But after a point you see where you're fucking up, what the conditioning has been.

Chrystos

I'm part Indian. I go to powwows sometimes and give-aways, and I take some Native American studies courses out at San Francisco State. I haven't gotten too involved with the group at State because it's very heterosexual, and I'm clear without even asking that it wouldn't be acceptable for me to be a dyke and also to be involved with them. So that's a tremendous conflict.

Although in quite a few of the cultures there used to be room for the men to be *heyokas*—they can dress like women and behave like women—there's really no space for women to be gay. For instance, I couldn't go to a powwow and dance with a woman lover during the couples' dance. As far as I know, there are only five or six Native American gay women on the West Coast, and there's only one other of them who is political in the sense that I am political, who wants to change things.

So I have a conflict that's really deep—between my cultural world, which fills some needs but doesn't allow me to be exactly who I am, and the lesbian world. I tend to stay in the lesbian world, because there's space for me to be part Indian in the lesbian world. Lesbians are so oppressed that everyone is acceptable, to some extent.

Canyon Sam

When I first came out, I wanted to find other Asian dykes. I didn't even know if there were any, but I knew that when

I saw lesbians in the cities, in the bars, at events, in the country, everywhere, they were all white. I started searching frantically to see if there were any other Asian women who had made that decision. I didn't find any.

I spent about six weeks in the city coming out before I went to the country. It was two years before I ever settled in the city again, which is where you're going to find Third World dykes. As long as I was living in the country, I couldn't expect to meet Asian dykes or Third World dykes. Finally, it got to a point where I knew that's what I needed, so I decided to leave the country and settle in the city.

Before I came out as a lesbian, I had been working with other young Asian Americans in a scene that was a nontraditional lifestyle. The traditional Asian way was to go onto math or sciences or engineering and be a wife and a mother. When I was in college, I met a new generation of Asian Americans who were artists, writers, and poets.

I was really close to that Asian group. They felt like a family to me because we were so united around our commonness as Asians. I knew that when I became a lesbian, I couldn't go back to that community because they were so blatantly heterosexual and sexist and into sex roles. They're into liberalness now, but they weren't then. The worst put-down the founder of the group had was he would call somebody a faggot when he got mad at them. Now, two years later, they're into this liberal trip. "Oh, we accept homosexuality. It's cool with us. Harvey's a homosexual." A token faggot. But they're straighter than straight.

White America has its hippie element and its new-age culture where people get looser. There are Asians who are like that, but they're in the larger white alternative community. There's not an Asian American community that is alternative and new-age hippie.

It was a very big dilemma. In the women's community,

there were no Asians; it was all white. In the Asian community, there were no lesbians and no feminists; it was a totally sexist and heterosexist scene. So basically what I did was I stayed with the women's community. That was stronger for me than having to be with the Asian Americans, because I was getting support as a woman and a lesbian.

But as I said, after a while it got to the point where I was fed up with the white Women's Movement. When I moved back to the city, it was with a commitment and a strong desire to organize Third World women and to meet and get support from other Third World women in the Women's Movement.

It's happened some, but it's really weird. Some of the personal connections I have made with other Third World dykes have been through mutual white friends. What happens, and it's happened with a lot of Third World dykes, is that when you first come out, you want to meet someone who's really your own kind. Not just lesbian, but also Black, or whatever. And then you put out and you put out and you put out and you don't find anyone, so you just get fed up and tired and you need support, anyway, so you go to other dykes, which means you start having a lot of non-Third World friends and lovers and social circles. Then through those people, you'll meet other Third World women who are in the same position of being isolated as Third World women around a lot of white women.

When I first got into the women's community, I thought, "Wow, lesbians!" All these people were giving me support for being a dyke, and it was just wonderful. I had a friend who was a Jewish woman. She was the first dyke I knew, and when I got together with her years later, she was into a total Jewish separatism dyke trip.

We got close, and then she said, "No. You have to be Jewish." I freaked out. I thought that was really oppressing

me as a non-Jewish woman. I said, "Why did you hang out
with me? Why did we get this close?" She said, "Well, at
least you're not white."

I thought that was totally fucked and oppressive, and one
time I told her that. She said, "Well, just think, Canyon.
What if you had an Asian lesbian feminist lover and she
shared so much of the parts of you? Have you ever stopped to
think about that? Isn't that a big difference from having a
lover who was a dyke but a WASP?"

I had *never* thought of that. All of a sudden, I became
illuminated as to what she was going through, wanting somebody who was also Jewish. I had never even let myself dream
that there could be another Asian dyke who had the same
experiences and consciousness and interests as I did. I just
took for granted that that would never exist, that all the
people I would be with in my life would be women and all
of them would be white.

Dolores Rodriguez

Right after I saw my reflection in the window and accepted
that I was a lesbian, I started to freak out. I was afraid of my
Chicano community rejecting me; not for what I wanted
to do, not for what I wanted to help in, but rejecting me for
being a lesbian. I was lucky, though, because that's when I
ran into these people who wanted to organize GALA (Gay
Latinos). That gave me something to work for.

This friend of mine told me, "You know tonight there's
going to be a bunch of gay Latinos meeting together." I
thought, "Far out." So me and four other women went, and
there was something like eighty people in there. Nobody
knew each other, and nobody knew where we were going to
start. Nobody knew who was going to run the meeting. But

here we were all together and we knew right then and there we weren't alone.

I related to that, because when I did start getting involved with other lesbians, I didn't hardly know any Latinas. The Latinas I knew were drinking and partying and dancing and just carrying on. I dug that, too, but there was something deeper I wanted to do.

The women I met who were concerned with gay rights and rap groups were all white. There was something empty in me. I thought, "Something about me isn't really blending. Yeah, we're women. Yeah, we're dykes. Yeah, we've been oppressed. Yeah, we had to come out. But there is still something deeper."

That's why I've stayed with GALA for so long. My main concern right now is the Chicano movement and how Chicanos and Chicanas relate to me. Half of them don't like the idea of homosexuality at all. But since I've been working with GALA, we're knocking down the walls slowly. That gives me hope that one day people are going to accept us. They're going to have to. We're all over. We're just coming out of the closet left and right.

Vera Freeman

When I was back home in Milwaukee this last time, my father rounded up some old friends I went to school with and said, "Vera's home; she's brought a woman with her."

It kind of upset my lover because a man came in the house and said, "Where's that white woman that Vera brought with her? Your father was up on the corner and told me that there was a white woman here."

Ghetto, right? Black ghetto. This man hadn't seen a white woman for miles, for years. My lover happened to be in the bathtub, but the man kept looking around to see if my father had lied.

Ana Torres

For a lot of women who are white, their first oppression is sexism or being lesbian. I don't live my life just as a lesbian. I don't see that as my first oppression, because I'm nonwhite. I see being a lesbian and being nonwhite as equally heavy oppressions in my life.

All my life I had this thing I had to deal with, because I don't look like a Chicana. I always felt really schizoid. "Wait a minute, how can I be Chicana if I don't look Chicana? I look white, and knowing that it's easier to be white, why don't I just be white? That way, I don't have to deal with telling people I'm Chicana and hearing people say, 'My, you don't *look* Chicana.' I don't have to deal with any kind of racism, and I don't have to deal with the fact that all my relatives live in Red Bluff and are very poor people and are incredibly discriminated against because of their skin. I can pass and be white."

In fact, until my third year of high school, I did pass. For the first two years of high school, I called myself Ann. The last two years, I changed my name back to Ana.

In the Chicano culture, like in all nonwhite cultures, the whiter you are, the better, because realistically you know that if you're whiter and you live in the U.S., you're going to make it. You're going to be able to get further along in school, and you're going to get a better job, and people are going to listen to you and respect you in a lot of subtle and a lot of real obvious ways.

When I would visit my cousins in Red Bluff, they would take me to see their other Chicano friends, and they'd say, "Look, this is my cousin! She looks really white, doesn't she?

But she's a Chicana!" They were really proud of the fact that I didn't look like a Chicana and that made me feel even worse. I mean, I knew what they were saying was good, but at the same time I wanted to look like my cousins, I wanted to be part of them so much.

After high school, I decided I didn't want to live a schizoid life anymore. I wanted to do things with Chicano people. So I joined MECHA, which is a Chicano organization. It was the first time I'd ever been around Chicanos in my life, other than my relatives. It was really hard because I met with a lot of the same kinds of attitudes. "What are you doing here? You're not really Chicana. You don't look like a Chicana, and you don't speak Spanish, so how could you really be?"

I was also always the one bringing up the sexist issues. "I'm willing to struggle as a Chicana, but not if I'm being treated sexist by you. I'm not willing to struggle with you if you look on me as any less than yourself." That was just taken like, "How dare you? You come in here and you look white and then you start spouting this women's lib stuff."

To the women I'd say, "We can't have the men telling us that they're more important than us. And we can't have men always speaking for us. We have to take part in that battle and be out there." But that was real hard, because part of me was feeling, "Maybe I should be quiet and suffer and be still," while the other part was feeling, "No. I'm not going to let go of those feminist values that I fought so hard to identify with, that made me feel like I'm sane and I make sense and I'm right."

I felt infinitely comfortable and uncomfortable at the same time. I just loved being there and hanging out with other Chicanas. "Yeah, these are my people, and I'm one of these people." I was learning a lot about my culture, things I had forgotten or things I had never been taught. A flood of memories would come back to me when I was there.

Also, for the first time in my life I felt incredibly loving

and sexual towards Chicano men. I think it was just because
I wanted so much to be part of that culture that I even fell
in love with the men and all their creepy sexist things.
There's something very wonderfully and also horribly appealing about Latino men. They have this wonderful nasty
sexual energy that, as women, we can just fall into. But then,
if I'd think about it, I'd go, "Wait a minute; that's horrible."

I started sort of being sexual with a Chicano, and it was a
wonderful experience. It was so totally different. I really
liked it. At that time, I hadn't started to come out as a
lesbian, but I was thinking about it a lot.

It was over the summer, after I finished at the junior college, that I came out as a lesbian. At the same time, I had a
job working with low income and minority kids in high
schools. Through my job, I had to make arrangements with
MECHA for field trips and orientations. I told the man I
had sort of started relating to at MECHA that I was a lesbian, and he was pissed at me. Telling him was one of the
stupidest things I've ever done because it was really threatening to him, and he just hated me for it.

I felt really threatened, too, because I thought he would
tell other people and my credibility would just be ruined.
I know that's the truth. People would have looked at me and
said, "Oh, she's just a lesbian, one of those women's libber
dykes." And they would not have believed anything I said or
had said. They would just have thought that all the work I
had done had somehow been wrong.

Here I was dealing with my lesbianism and dealing with
coming out, and then having to go to work and be this heavy-
duty Chicana who was doing peer counseling with other
Chicanas. It was really hard going to work and putting on
this facade. It was two different cultures: lesbian woman
culture and Chicano culture.

It was hard to think that something so wonderful and life-
giving as loving a woman would be seen as so horrible and

negative by a group of people. That's the part I really hate about my culture. It's so homophobic. In a lot of ways, I'll never be accepted by the majority of Chicanos or Chicanas. That's a reality that I have to live with.

At this job we would sponsor dances, and people would ask me, "Where's your boyfriend?" I would say, "I'm not relating to men right now." A lot of the young women could relate to that, because they'd really been fucked over by men and also had a lot of ideas about what men were through their mothers. That's really a cultural thing with Chicanas and Latinas. You learn a lot about men and their values through your mother. There's this particular thing about Latino men that they're not very trustworthy but they're great lovers. They'll probably treat you real bad, but that's your lot in life. So when I told them I wasn't relating to men, they didn't think it was weird; they just thought, "Well, she'll relate to men later on; she's just burned out." So I was covered there, but I was also fearful because I was working in a school district. With me being a lesbian and working with high school students, the program would have been eliminated if anyone had found out. So it was real scary.

I have felt a lot of pressure from women saying it was my duty as a lesbian and as a feminist to come out to everybody, and that includes my parents. That's how you change people's attitudes about lesbianism. I agree with that, but there's another part of me that knows those are class values and cultural values about how you deal with your parents and what you tell your parents. I feel strongly that my parents know I'm a lesbian, but we could never speak those words. We don't tell each other a lot about our changes. What they connect lesbianism with is a lot of sexual stuff, and so for them it would automatically mean perverseness and not all the stuff that lesbianism means to me. They wouldn't see it as a real political choice in my life, as something important and not just a sexual choice.

Somehow it would be disrespectful to say to them, "Look, I'm a lesbian, and you're going to have to deal with it." I don't have the right to do that. They've been through so much in their lives about being Chicanos and living in this society. They've just taken so much shit that I won't do that to them until I feel like it can be said.

Now I'm focusing a lot on being nonwhite and rediscovering what that means for me, trying to figure out how I'll work out my politics. Lately, a lot of my oppression hasn't been around being lesbian, because I live around a large community of women, I'm involved in women's studies at school, and I go to school—which is a safe environment. I see as my main struggle in life how to synthesize being a Chicana and also being a strong feminist and a lesbian; how to work those out and how to reach other nonwhite women; how to make white women aware that we need to support other nonwhite people's struggles as much as we need nonwhite women to be in the Women's Movement. We need to support those people and then ask them for their support, too.

I'm twenty-two. I grew up in Santa Barbara. Both my parents grew up in New Mexico and came to California after the war. My father works on a loading dock, and my mom's worked since she was fourteen, mostly as a bookkeeper. They have a middle-class income now, although they still identify as working class and have those values. I'm a poet, and that's what I want to do in my life.

Lesbian Community

As you begin to explore your lesbian identity, a crucial question is often: How do you find other lesbians you can relate to and get support from? Is there a "lesbian community"? If so, will you feel comfortable in that community? The women here used different strategies to find other lesbians, and they have a variety of feelings about their communities.

You will also meet a new woman, Cindy, in this final chapter who will describe how the lesbian culture and the local lesbian community influenced her coming out process and continue to influence her life today.

Carol Queen

I tried to get in touch with the lesbian community before I even felt I could call myself a lesbian. I went to the Gay

People's Alliance office, to the lesbian rap group, to all the events at Gay Pride Week, and to a gay studies class.

After I felt I could call myself gay, I joined a bisexual women's rap group and made a lot of good friends there.

Since Gay Youth got started almost a year ago, my friends are almost all gay. I was one of the two people who founded it, and it's grown from those two people to about forty-five full members now. As many as seventy-five or eighty people come out of the woodwork like you wouldn't believe if we throw a party. These are mostly people under twenty-three. It's provided the kind of support group that I certainly never had when I was in high school and just out of high school. It's a lot more open about gayness and about each member's sexuality than anybody ever was before. It's really a welcome thing to have. I'm not saying that because I founded it; I'm saying that because it meets a personal need in me, too. I wish somebody had founded it a long time ago.

Laverne Jefferson

I did three years in jail. My lover got out of jail before I did, and she waited for me, and then we just settled down. At that time, there wasn't very many gay people around. The people I hung around with was mostly straight. This was '72, '73. I didn't have any reason to find gay people because I was busy helping my family out, going to work, working on getting my son Tommy back. I was just into getting my own self together. I did meet some people through my therapist, and then a couple of years later, I started going to the gay bar and meeting people.

What I've had hard in this community is being the only Black gay female. I can't get in with the gay women here. I just feel like I'm the only one on the earth, because they can't deal with me and they can't understand me. I've had more trouble out of the lesbian women here for being gay than I've had out of the straight community.

A lot of ladies in the women's bar, if they see me come in there with a white lady, they just look at me. There was maybe three Black people in the bar the other night from out of town, and a lot of the women would just sit and stare at the white women that were with them. That's why I don't want to stay here.

If someone does go to bed with me in this town, the other lesbians give them a bad name. They gave this one lady such a bad name that she went straight. I swear to God. Now they're all sitting in the bar talking about how this lady they know went straight. But they did it to her.

Not too long ago, all I had was that one friend. She'd come over, and we'd talk and get drunk and go to the city and party because we couldn't party here. And so they all got down on her. She'd say, "Wow, why are the women doing this shit? I found men that treat me better than this." I said, "Yeah, I know what you mean."

We were discussing about going straight; then she did and I didn't. The gay community drove her to the point where she went straight, but they don't know it. And she was a Filipino lady. Pissed me off. I really support her because these women here, some of them can drive you crazy. They haven't seen that many Black women in this community or that many Filipinos, and they don't know how to deal with us.

Jeri

The first two years Rose and I were together, we didn't know another gay person. We had no support from anybody and we were miserable. We were living in Hawaii at the time, and we grew to hate the place just because of what it represented to us. It was a prison, self-imposed, maybe, but nevertheless a prison. We finally reached the conclusion that it was time to meet some other gay people; so we moved to San Francisco.

After we'd lived in San Francisco a year, we still didn't know where any gay bars or groups were. We just didn't know how to make contact. Then one day we saw an article about a lesbian in the *Chronicle*, and it mentioned Daughters of Bilitis. So we quick got out the Yellow Pages, and sure enough, there it was. We just went through the ceiling.

We got all dressed up in skirts and earrings to go to the first meeting. We got to the elevator, and I told Rose, "I can't do it. I just can't do it. I'm going to die. I've got the feeling I'm going to meet somebody there that I know." I was almost in tears. Finally, she dragged me in the elevator, and we got up to the door. I would have sold my soul not to go in. We walked into the room, and it was full of women in sweatshirts and jeans and tennis shoes.

Anyway, we got through the meeting okay. It was a neat experience but really heavy, just being there with lesbians. I couldn't believe it. It didn't meet in any secret dungeon. It was kind of a dinky office, but it wasn't any secret meeting place.

When the meeting was almost over, I was starting to feel relaxed, and in walks this woman and her friend. I took one look and almost fell through the floor. She was one of my clients. I was doing auditing for an accounting firm, and she happened to work for one of my clients. I thought the world was going to end right there. Well, she was surprised to see me, and I was surprised to see her. Then it dawned on both of us. "What's the other one doing here?"

We had a good laugh about it after the meeting. She took us to our first gay bar. It was hilarious to find out that her boss was gay and the guy I went auditing with was also gay. The two dykes and the two queens.

Rose and I became active in the Daughters of Bilitis. It was like a whole new world opening up to us to find out that some of our feelings were the same feelings other women were dealing with, and to start feeling better about ourselves. It was exciting to find out who we were and to share some of the common problems and the common victories in our lives.

Maria Gonzales

When I came back from Puerto Rico, that's when the feminist movement started: 1969, 1970. All of these women are coming out, and I'm loving it. But they're coming out in a different sense—not like I came out, that was for sure. They had this consciousness of going through a lot of shit and coming out of it. My coming out was very blunt. Hey, they're women, I like women, boom. These are the reasons why, very clear.

All of a sudden, *lesbians* are telling me that I'm wrong for the way I feel about other women. Me? I've been out since I was seven. I've been making love to women since I was seven. "Oh, you're only after women for sex." That ain't true. Because I say, "Oh, she sure looks hot," that means I'm after her body, all of a sudden!

If I'd be cruising a woman or something, somebody would say, "Hey, that's sleazy." "What do you mean, it's sleazy? Why can't I enjoy that? Why can't I do that? What are you telling me—that it's wrong for me to see a really good-looking woman who turns me on and say she's a really good-looking woman who turns me on?"

I said to this one woman, "Oh, God, you're cute." "Cute!

Don't call me cute. Men have been calling me cute all my life." I said, "I'm not a man." I have a lot of friends who are lesbians, and I say, "Hey, cutie this and cutie that." That doesn't mean that I'm being oppressive.

All of a sudden, I have to find a new language to speak, just because our language has been made up by men. That's stupid. To me, that's just getting a little ridiculous, going overboard with an issue. There are times when people can get into semantics and get really petty about what you say, what you do, how you present yourself.

Chrystos

Acceptance within the lesbian community has been the biggest conflict for me, because I have very long hair, and there are a lot of very feminine things—like lace curtains and long hair—that I don't want to give up. I don't want to run around in Levi's jackets and work boots for the rest of my life and not have any of those other parts of myself that I really enjoy. In this particular community, there's a lot of hostility to keeping all those parts of yourself. For instance, a woman said to me once that having long hair was a heterosexual privilege that allowed me to go through the community without being hassled.

I'm slowly realizing that when a lot of women first come out, they're functioning under a lot of anger. I didn't come out because of anger at men; I was just disgusted with them. It was hopeless. Whatever anger I did have against men— and it's still there when they hassle me on the streets—is not of the intensity that a lot of women feel. So I'm probably more mellow about being gay and more flexible and tolerant. I feel like anybody who wants to be a dyke can be a dyke. They don't have to cut their hair or even necessarily be feminists, which is another way I'm different from a lot of

women. I don't feel that all women who are gay are feminists. I know they aren't. So I don't see why that should be
any kind of criterion.

Esther Brown

One of the things that postpones women's coming out is
their exposure to a bad element of the lesbian community.
Back in the beginning days, we called them bull dykes, and
it wasn't a pleasant term. They swaggered around, walked
like men, dressed like men, wore black leather jackets, and
would fight at the drop of a hat.

I was exposed to that. I thought, "Well, crap. I don't
want any part of that." Around Anchorage, it was just terrible because they'd go around in gangs. They'd fight men;
they'd fight anybody. That type of exposure is going to dis-
courage women who are very sincere and want to be with
other women but just can't hack it because of these bull
dykes.

In my way of thinking, that is a definite class within the
lesbian structure. You have your classes in this way of life
just like you do in any other form of society. Your coming
out depends not only on where you are, but also on who
you meet and how you meet them.

I met other women through sports. I played golf; I
bowled. And, of course, you know they are lesbians. It's the
unspoken word, but you just have a sixth sense that they
are, or if they aren't they should be because of their ex-
pressions, their interests. And then it just more or less de-
velops that you associate with them.

Now that I live down here in Washington, the ranch takes
up a great deal of my time, and I'm kind of complacent. I get
up in the morning, and I'm just elated to be here. If Seattle
weren't the closest metropolitan area, I'd probably be just

going my merry little way, content to be by myself, and going to the local potlucks with straight people.

This city is more relaxed, as far as lesbianism, than any other city I've been around. Here there are so many ways to meet lesbians, because they have so any women things going. They have music; they have poetry readings. All you have to do is just attend. In '74, I started coaching a women's softball team in Seattle, and that's how I got acquainted with a lot of women.

Rose

During high school, I didn't find any gay people to relate to, exactly. I was just searching. When I used to work at a drive-in restaurant, I worked with some girls who really liked to tease with the boys. We used to have contests to see who could flirt the most with whom. Well, I used to flirt with men and women, too. This was before I met Jeri.   .

This one night, I was flirting with this woman, and she had a girlfriend with her. She was an older woman. I was just talking with her and being really neat with her. I didn't realize, for some reason or other, that she was gay. I don't know why. Maybe because I was working and I wasn't really paying any attention to the person herself, but because the person was there, I was just being friendly with her. I was looking for gay people, but I don't know how come it didn't even dawn on me until she left. While she was still there, she asked me to go out on a date with her. I said, "Sure, I'll go out with you." Her girlfriend was really jealous. Her girlfriend says," You don't want to go out with her. She's no good." I said, "How do I know? I don't even know the person." She was quite a bit older than I was, because at the time I was seventeen.

So she goes to a bar, I guess, or someplace, and she called

me up at work. Well, see, in the meantime, while she was gone, I knew better, because that's what I was, also, but the people at work said, "You don't want to go out with her because she likes women." And I said, "So what? No big deal." But then they started kind of making fun of it. So when she called up, I told her, "I can't go out with you. I have this boyfriend and blah, blah, blah." I was making all this crap up, which was really dumb, what I was doing. She said, "Well, is he stronger than I am?" And I said, "Oh, yes, five times stronger."

Now, here's another dumb thing. I was so tickled that she asked me out that I go home and I tell my mother; I tell my father; I tell everybody. I even told my aunt. She said, "You know there are some women that like women, too." I said, "I know! I know!" I was just so tickled, I was floating on air. And then, oh, I kick myself for not actually going. Well, you see, I probably couldn't have gone out with her, anyway, unless I snuck out of the house. My parents wouldn't have let me go out with her, and that's really mainly why I did that. I think if she was younger, I probably would have had a better chance even to go to a movie with her.

Later, I was working with my brother's ex-girlfriend, and she always used to tell me how I should meet Jeri, because she was a neat person to get to know and to have as a friend. She never thought anything else, of course. So one day, by accident, we did meet, and, well, it was love at first sight.

Jeri and I didn't stay in Oregon for very long; we ran away to Hawaii. Social life over there wasn't too good because we didn't know any gay people, and I didn't like straight people. I get uptight. Straight people are really straight people. If there's straight people that you can just deal with and talk with and have some fun with, they're fine, but some straight people are really a bore. I think, anyway. So we really didn't have much of a social life.

Then we moved to San Francisco, and that's when our

social life started, because I started looking for gay clubs or gay people, and I started searching them out. Jeri was having a really hard time being gay, so I thought if she was around other gay people, it would be easier on her. It was pretty hard.

Canyon Sam

I had some vague notion of what the women's community was. I knew it existed somewhere because of all the women's liberation stuff in the late sixties and early seventies when I was junior-high-school age. So I made a couple of attempts at trying to break into the San Francisco women's community, and they were real failures.

I knew one dyke, just one. She told me about this bar where I'd find other Asian dykes. Here I had just turned nineteen, so innocent in many ways. I looked in the Muni schedule and found out how to get the buses to this strange part of town. I went in the night, took three transfers, and waited in the wind. It was dark, and I was in a part of the city that I didn't know. Finally, I found this bar that looked like a sleazy place. I was scared.

I went up the stairs and was going to try to slip in, but I didn't have an ID and they caught me. I was just at the top of the stairs and the whole room was packed. There must have been two hundred women there. I was going, "Wow, look, it's all women. Wow, they're all dancing with each other. Wow, wow, wow, look at all this energy; it's just women."

I was standing there and they were hassling me, flashing around their flashlights and hustling me down the stairs. I was saying, "Wait, wait. Can I maybe just stand here and watch for a while?" They said, "No, come on, get." They were really cold and awful. Here I thought I was coming into

this women's community which was going to be so loving
and supportive and sisterhood—all this stuff I heard when I
was a straight woman, and they were total pigs. They practically threw me down the stairs. When I didn't get anywhere
with that, I just had to take the buses all the way home for
another hour and a half.

Next, I saw this announcement of a gay rap in the Gay
Life column of the *Bay Guardian*. On that Wednesday night,
I took long bus rides and transfers and was real scared going
alone to this gay rap. I went up to the fourth floor of a big
building, opened the auditorium doors, and there were seventy-five gay men all sitting around talking. That's the kind
of thing that happened to me.

I also tried to get into another bar, and I did get in even
without an ID, but I didn't know how to do the bar scene.
How do you approach people you are interested in? What do
you say? "How often do you come here?" or "What's your
name; what do you do?" It was so phony. I just couldn't relate to it. I would end up playing the pinball machine.

At this time, I was not in touch with the women's community as far as knowing about *Plexus,* or women's centers, or
coming-out groups, or support groups. I was also totally
weirded out by the city, so I decided to move to Oregon. I
went to a country retreat run by women in southern Oregon
and found a whole community of women there.

After being with some country lesbians for a while, I had a
dream where I knew I wanted to be one of these women.
There was a huge warehouse, very white and sparkling. I
saw conveyor belts that were all twisted and went around
each other like an entanglement of roller coasters. They were
little assembly lines carrying these brightly colored blocks
squeezed right next to each other. They were wonderful
colors, but they were all just chugging along on these lines,
with walls right on their sides so you didn't have room to
move; you just followed the one right in front of you.

I interpreted that dream as my fear of being one of the gang. When you're a country lesbian, you dress in baggy, dirty pants; you cut your hair in this way; you smoke dope; you have this political rhetoric line; you know how to do carpentry. I freaked out that I would lose my individualism because of a group identity. But I also saw that it was not entirely bad, because those assembly lines sometimes went on rides and swung around freely, and it was fun. I saw those things as being beautiful, but I felt a constriction at the same time.

Jane Salter

While I was still living with a man, I was already in love with a woman, so I knew a lot of women because I hung out with her. I started taking women's classes at U.C. Berkeley and met lots of women there. Then five of us from Berkeley started a women's coffeehouse, and I met lots and lots and lots of women. My lack of sight has been difficult because it was intimidating to some people at the coffeehouse, but I'm very extroverted; I always have been. I've always had a lot of people around me and a lot of friends. That's been very important to me.

I remember one woman I was going out with said, "Do you ever go to movies?" I said, "Yeah, if they're not subtitled, and they ought to let me in half-price."

I'm very self-protective. I go places with people I trust, or I go to familiar places where either I know how to leave by myself or where someone's with me. I was just up in Vancouver, and I went to a mixed gay bar with a woman friend. We were with some gay men we had met in the street. One of the gay men was drunk and kept pinching my ass and my tits and wouldn't leave me alone. In this city, it would never happen. I asked him to stop, I told him to stop, and then I started a fight. I didn't know how to get out of the bar, it was huge. I couldn't just go to a phone and call someone to pick me up. My friend was off dancing, and I ended up getting slapped in the mouth for the first time in my life. It was an accident, but still it happened and it flipped me out. I was real angry. Had I been here, I would have gotten up and left.

I get to feeling, I don't know how else to put it, but very femmie a lot of times on people's arms, having the kind of dependence I have on them in awkward situations. That's real heavy for me. I've been independent since I was twelve, and I don't like the dependence I have.

At one point, I decided I would do everything myself. But suddenly I realized I was devoting my life to being blind. It would take me all day to do the shopping and the laundry, and it wasn't worth it. There are too many things I have to do in my life. I work very hard at the coffeehouse, I write poetry, and I'm finishing my master's. I cannot do all those things without a lot of help. I'm fortunate that there are many women willing to help me live my life.

Dolores Rodriguez

In high school, I just knew a couple of lesbians. Then after high school, I moved to Sacramento and I started going to gay bars. It was a trip. I felt like I was in straight life and I was doing what I had always dreamed of doing: to dress in men's clothes and have short hair and have a girlfriend with makeup and earrings and dresses.

Carol Gay

When I started thinking of myself as a lesbian, I started hanging out down at the gay bar. There was one gay bar in Mobile where there were usually about sixty men and five to ten women. Most of the women were into heavy roles. I'd walk in and see this big butch bull dyke and get scared out of my mind and think, "I don't want to be a lesbian. I don't want to go in there."

I remember the first time I went to the bar. My roommate Paula took me. I walked in, and these heavy bull dykes were all sitting around one table with their arms folded. My heart just dropped to the floor, and I thought, "God, what do I do if one of them asks me to dance?" I danced. I was scared to say no.

The only exposure I'd ever had to lesbians was through the lesbian feminists in my CR group who were non-role-playing, regular people. I tried not to get too freaked out in the bar because I'd heard about the stereotypes, and I knew, "Well, that's them." It was strange to see women trying to act like men, because I had been exposed through lesbian-feminists instead of through such heavy types, and I couldn't connect the two.

I did hang out there all year, and I would talk to the women to try to find out where their heads were, rolewise. One of them said, "I act like a man and I dress like a man because that's what you have to do to get women." It made a lot of sense, since they had never had any other roles to go by.

For all Mobile doesn't have, it does have closeness among the gay people because there are so few and they're so harassed. The first night I went to the gay bar, four or five gay men invited me over for dinner and said, "It's really great that you're here." That made it even easier to come out because here were all these supportive, warm people. Within a short time, I had ten or fifteen good gay friends.

I happened to meet three or four women who were in-between. They weren't heavy role-players, but they didn't know anything about feminism because the one CR group in Mobile had not hit a lot of people. So I hung out at the bar with them for a year, thinking, "I know I'm a lesbian now, but what's wrong with me that I don't want to go to bed with these women? I just can't make it here. They're all into roles, and they don't know what I'm talking about when I tell them not to sexualize me."

At one point, I went to a lesbian convention in Birmingham because I thought it would be different in the big city. But I got to the big city, and they were playing the same games. So I decided to leave the South and to start traveling in search of women I could relate to. I was going crazy with isolation. I ended up in San Francisco about two years ago and said, "Aha! Mecca! Gee, there are more than two of them here."

Vera Freeman

I had no problem, because somebody took me around and introduced me to the gay bars. The bars were the only place you could go to be with other women. I didn't like the bar scene in those days. It was pretty harsh.

I was considered that amazing woman, because I was married and here I was going out to be with other women and how did I manage it? I knew some pretty nice women. They didn't make demands on my time. They respected that I believed in taking care of my children and having them with me most of the time, except, of course, when I was out at night at the bar. If I was strapped for a sitter, they would see that I could get a sitter so I could be with them.

I hear women saying how difficult it is for them to get somebody to keep their kids for them so they can get their schooling, get off welfare, and go to work. I didn't have that problem because these women were all willing to do it for me. If they had kids, I could do it in turn for them. So being gay has its benefits, really. Compare it to the heterosexual world where they always have to be shelling out money for baby-sitters.

Mary Howland

Once I knew I was a lesbian, I realized that the small redneck farm town where I lived was not a good place to come out. It was also not a good place to get the emotional support that I needed growing up lesbian at thirty-six years old. It was almost a whole year from the time I had my first sexual experience to the time I actually moved into Minneapolis. In the meantime, I socialized with two or three friends that I knew were lesbians and asked them to refer me to good lesbian literature. I was just really feeling great.

When I got to Minneapolis, I made contact with the lesbian women I knew and said, "Being a person who never even dated heterosexually much, I don't know how to go about things. How do I get started?" It was really dumb at thirty-six years old to say, "Tell me how." I said, "Where are the gay people?" They said, "Of course, they're all over, but they're not going to tell you."

These friends were very, very nice. They took me to several house parties and garden parties of gay teachers and nurses where I met some people, and it was exciting. I loved it. One of them took me on a tour of the bars and gave me some helpful pointers. I was highly impressed with one thing, and I continue to be. That is, that in a gay bar, I am far less hassled and hustled and degraded by either men or women than I was in a straight bar. I have yet to have a demeaning or upsetting experience in a gay bar, and I've been in gay bars in several cities now.

Olivia Moreno

I met my first lover here at the college. Then, when I was eighteen, I went to the Gay People's Alliance office, and they gave me the number of Gay Youth. I met a lot of people through Gay Youth. Coming out was a really easy thing for me to do. It's a bummer that you have to be twenty-one to go into the gay bar because that's where you meet a lot of people, but we have parties and stuff at Gay Youth.

If I was still living in Cathlamet, I wouldn't be out hardly at all. Cathlamet is pretty conservative.

Jacqueline Denton

I had already found out about the lesbian subculture through the women's support groups I was in before I came out myself. I knew lesbians in the groups, and there are a couple of lesbians who conduct groups for lesbians.

I knew there were some gay bars, although I hadn't gone until Sandra took me the first time.

Cindy

The lesbian community and lesbian culture, especially women's music, really helped me come out. The first women's album I bought was "Face the Music" by Meg Christian; then I bought Linda Shear's album, "A Lesbian Portrait." I was afraid to buy Linda's album because Linda makes it clear she doesn't want any straight women listening to her album, and I thought the woman at the counter of the bookstore would know I hadn't decided to be a lesbian yet. I listened to that album over and over and over again, and read and reread her album cover.

Linda says as long as you collaborate with the enemy, and we do have to realize men are the enemy, you're not doing anybody any good; you're working within their systems. You have to get out of their systems in order to win over. She also really loves women a lot, and the positiveness of her thoughts attracted me. She talks about goddesses and the family of woman. She's very strong. She says what she believes, and she says right out, "A lot of women are going to hate me for what I say, but this is what I believe and I have to say it." I got a lot of my lesbian separatist beliefs from Linda Shear. It didn't make any sense to be a lesbian and not be a separatist, so when I did come out as a lesbian, I came out as a lesbian separatist.

The night I actually decided to come out I went to a solstice party that was only women, and when you go to anything that's all women, the majority are lesbians. I saw women hanging out with each other and not needing men around at all, and I just started feeling really good about the women in the lesbian community. They seemed to be so free.

I also talked to a lot of lesbians that night about the theater group they were in or about this or that, and I started seeing that there was a real lesbian community. The community part attracted me more than anything else. These women obviously hung out together, knew each other quite well, and loved each other a lot. I really liked that because in the heterosexual world I don't think there's too much chance for a real community feeling; everybody's so busy competing with everybody else for different things. At this party I didn't notice too much competition. Now that I'm more a part of the community I can see little things, "She took my lover away from me, blah blah blah . . ." but there's so much less of that than there is in the heterosexual community. So it was the sharing, the love, that just amazed me. I thought, "Yeah, I can come out into this. These women will take care of me."

At the party I sat and watched two women make out for a long time. It was the first time I'd ever done that. I could do it because it was dark so I wasn't noticed watching them. The previous summer I had said to my mom, "I don't know

now anyone could kiss someone of the same sex, but I don't see why they should be persecuted." At this party I still didn't think I could do it myself, but I watched these women be really in love with each other and that attracted me.

I didn't actually decide to be a lesbian until I got home that night. I was sitting in my chair listening to women's music, and a male friend of mine came in to talk to me. I told him that I didn't know if he could understand, but I was real happy because I had just decided to be a lesbian.

After that the people in my co-op house hated me, I was so out. I didn't see any sense in being a lesbian and not being out about it. The whole point, to me, of being a lesbian was to make a point, so I had to make it.

When I first came out I didn't really know of any dyke—only things going on because I came out in East Lansing, and East Lansing had feminist events rather than lesbian events. I did know that there was a Lesbian Center in Lansing, however, so a friend, Debi, and I went to it for the New Year's Eve party and were quite nervous. It was my big step.

I knew a few women there who were in a radical feminist group that I was in, so I talked to them. I also got my first kiss from a woman and was very thrilled because she gave me a French kiss, and I'd never been French-kissed by a woman before. I remember announcing to Debi, "Wow! She French-kissed me!" This year I went around and made a point of kissing everybody, but not that year. I was very shy.

The Lesbian Center was a lot different than I thought it would be. You see, I thought from the solstice party that all lesbians liked each other and cared about each other and hung out together. I found out at the New Year's Eve party that wasn't true. The Center's a lot different from a personal party. At the Center you have a lot of women who don't know each other, and a lot of women who come from out of town.

So I felt kind of lonely that night, as if I didn't know if I was ever going to get to know these women. It was very frightening that not a whole lot of women were coming up and talking to me. They weren't saying, "Wow, who are you? You're new! I haven't seen you around here." It wasn't the way I had expected it to be. I was disappointed.

I came to find out later that Debi and I had quite a reputation around town. People knew who we were, but we didn't know who they were. We were living with straight women who had these feminist lesbian friends who couldn't understand where Debi and I were coming from in being so separatist. I even talk to them now and they say, "Oh yeah, I heard about you. The first time I heard about you was when you confronted Jane about the politics of the women's restaurant." That's the kind of gossip that gets passed around, and that might be why people didn't come up and introduce themselves to us.

Debi and I also kind of clung to each other. We were thought by many to be lovers, and I've noticed that if two women walk into a party and they're lovers, a lot of people will leave them alone.

Debi and I had zero friends for about three months. We didn't know anybody. We read a lot; I came out in some of my classes and met a couple of lesbians that way. We went to the Lesbian Center, and we started going to the bar on Thursday nights, women's night.

No great friendships of mine ever started at the bar, but it was a very free place to go because you could sit back and watch lesbians be together. At the Lesbian Center we went to dances mostly, and potlucks, social things. We always left early, though, because the party never really starts until late and that's when all the people who know each other are there.

I didn't really get to know the community until five months after the New Year's Eve party when I moved out of East Lansing, into Lansing, and into an established lesbian household. It was actually living with lesbians that did it. I recommend it for every lesbian. I really do. Living in that house, I found that the lesbian community was much vaster than I'd ever thought it was. I met women who had lived in Lansing and been lesbians for ten, fifteen years. I started to know women who worked in factories. I never realized there were so many lesbians and so many different kinds of lesbians.

We had many many many political discussions on the porch of my house that summer. I didn't work all summer; I just sat on the porch and tons of people came. That's how I got to know most of the women I know now—just by them coming and visiting when they saw somebody sitting on the porch. I got to know enough women so that when I went to an event, I felt comfortable. I wasn't an outsider anymore.

Also, when I moved into that house, I came out sexually. I'm sure that helped me feel more a part of the community. I had come out in December, but I didn't sleep with a woman until May, and, for a couple of months before May, I had gotten accused by some straight women of not really being a lesbian because I hadn't slept with a woman. I started feeling that maybe I needed to justify my lesbianism. So it helped to sleep with a woman.

Later that summer I went to the Michigan Womyn's Music Festival for the first time. I got a whole different perspective on lesbian culture because a wide spectrum of viewpoints was represented there. I'd never been with that many lesbians in my life before; I think there were six thousand. It was quite a shock seeing so many women all at once.

There was a lot of nudity and a lot of women feeling free. For the first time in my life I walked somewhere without being in fear. I was walking to my tent from one of the concerts one night and I started to get scared. Suddenly I realized, "I don't have to be scared here."

I've never regretted my decision to be a lesbian. I think once a woman gets to a certain point of awareness she can't go back, and I guess I've reached that point. I couldn't go back politically; I couldn't go back personally.

Lansing is the perfect place for would-be lesbians because there are lots of concerts and lesbian events and women's events you can go to and watch lesbians hang out together. We have a women's chorus that's all lesbian; there's a women's T.V. show, *Woman Wise,* that's run by lesbians; and there's a lesbian feminist radio show called Womyn's Voice. The *Lesbian Connection* magazine comes out of Lansing. We have a dyke basketball team, and we had two dyke softball teams this summer in the city leagues. Now we have the lesbian theater collective. We've had a Lesbian Political Action Conference here. We've had a softball tournament to raise money for the dyke musical and four whole softball teams full of dykes played in it.

I'm tremendously busy. Keeping the Lesbian Center alive takes a lot of work, and I worked on that collective for a while. I go to a lot of meetings. We Lansing dykes have meetings down, we decided. We came out of a meeting the other night and one of the women said, "Wow, we did that meeting in an hour." We all know what we're going to talk about; we take our tasks; at the end of the meeting we go around and say what we're going to do that week, and then we're done. We're just really good at meetings, so we do a lot of meetings in Lansing.

One woman, who's part of Mellow Muse, the women's production company collective, said she moved here from Maine because she'd heard about the lesbian community. She said a lot of lesbians come here because they hear about it, and then they end up staying. I know two native Lansing-ites. Everyone else I know has moved here.

I have thought many times about moving, but I'm probably going to end up staying in Lansing for the rest of my life because of the women's community. My number one priority in moving anywhere is the community, and if I can't find something as good as this, I'm certainly not going to move. I feel like these women are my family. I guess I'm in love with the community, and I think a lot of other women are.

It's really important to remember that the community is not something out there. It takes a lot of individual work to make a community good, and I believe there are many responsibilities lesbians have to their communities to keep those communities alive and good and active. All too often a lot of us just sit back and think the community will entertain us, or the community will make our lives good, when in reality the community is us. It is our individual lives all put together. It can't be reduced to one sentence of, "We are responsible for our community," but it's the most important thing that we all have to remember.

———

I'm twenty-five; I'm white; I'm middle class. I grew up basically in the Midwest. My father was an engineer; my mother was a housewife and worked at places like Woolworth's sometimes. My father didn't live with us a lot. I was never forced to do too many things that I didn't want to do. I admire my parents for that. I had a lot of choice in my life, and I think that helped me be independent.

I work in a print shop. I go to a lot of meetings, and I'm very involved in the lesbian theater collective right now. That's my main project.

Your Community

Support and information are crucial aids for dealing with any lesbian crossroad. This list of information sources was updated in 1988 and should help you find your community wherever you are. Don't forget to send a stamped, self-addressed, business-size envelope if you want a reply.

Resource Lists

Gaia's Guide, 15 W. 44th St., New York, N.Y. 10036. A listing of lesbian restaurants, accommodations, bars, bookstores, services and organizations in the United States, Canada, Europe, Australia and New Zealand. It comes out yearly with updated entries and includes national organizations, publications and mail-order houses. Order from Giovanni's Room, 345 S. 12th St., N.E., Philadelphia, PA 19107. (800) 222-6996.

Gayellow Pages, Renaissance House, Box 292, Village Station, New York, NY 10014. (212) 674-0120. A guide to accommodations, bars, churches, healthcare, businesses, publications and organizations in the United States and Canada. Updated yearly.

Index/Directory of Women's Media, 3306 Ross Place, N.W., Washington, D.C. 20008. (202) 966-7783. Listing of women's periodicals, presses, bookstores and groups.

Womyn's Braille Press, Inc., Box 8475, Minneapolis, MN 55408.
(612) 822-0549. Feminist and lesbian literature in braille or
recorded format.

National Women's Mailing List — from the Women's
Information Exchange, 1195 Valencia St., San Francisco, CA
94110. (415) 824-6800. You can sign up to get information on
lesbians, women's health, art, politics and much more.

International Advisory Council for Homosexual Men & Women
in Alcoholics Anonymous, Box 492 Village Station, New York,
NY 10014. World Directory of gay/lesbian groups, issued to
alcoholics only.

National Association of Lesbian and Gay Alcoholism
Professionals (NALGAP), 204 W. 20th St., New York, NY
10011. (212) 807-0634. Directory of Facilities and Services for
Gay/Lesbian Alcoholics.

Homosexual Information Center, 6758 Hollywood Blvd. #208,
Los Angeles, CA 90028. (213) 464-8431. Publishes a Directory of
Homosexual Organizations and Publications.

International Directory of Gay and Lesbian Periodicals, Oryx
Press, 2214 N. Central Ave. #103, Phoenix, AZ 85004. (602)
254-6156.

The Lesbian Connection, P.O. Box 811, East Lansing, MI 48823.
Magazine with grass roots lesbian news from all over the
country. Includes a list of contact dykes who can be contacted
about resources in their areas of the country. Also lists current
events, restaurants, stores, organizations, women's land,
publications, books and miscellany.

The Wishing Well, P.O. Drawer G, Santee, CA 92071. A personal
contact club and magazine for lesbians who want to correspond
with and meet other lesbians with similar interests.

Referral Sources

National Gay/Lesbian Crisisline, 666 Broadway, 6th floor, New York, NY 10012. In New York: (212) 529-1604; all others (800) 221-7044, M–F 5–10 PM, Sat. 1–5 PM EST. Nationwide gay and lesbian referrals to local hotlines and support services, crisis intervention and phone counseling, national aids counseling line.

National Gay & Lesbian Task Force, 1517 U St. N.W., Washington, DC 20009. (202) 332-6483. Promotes gay civil rights legislation and acts as a clearinghouse for the national gay rights movement. Puts out a quarterly newsletter and has listings for lesbian and gay services across the U.S.

Midwest Committee for Military Counseling, 421 S. Wabash Ave. #200, Chicago, IL 60605-1208. (312) 939-3349. Legal referrals and counseling for lesbian and gay military, veterans, and draft-age gay men.

National Lawyers Guild Gay Caucus, 558 Capp St., San Francisco, CA 94110. (415) 285-5066. Legal support and referrals.

National Organization for Women, Inc., 1401 New York Ave. N.W. #800, Washington, DC 20005. (202) 347-2279. Largest women's rights organization in the U.S. Very active in lesbian rights. Some local chapters have lesbian task forces.

Religious and Ethnic Groups

Conference for Catholic Lesbians, Box 436 Planetarium Station, New York, NY 10024. (212) 595-2768. National network of local groups and contacts.
International Conference of Gay & Lesbian Jews, Box 881272, San Francisco, CA 94188.

Universal Fellowship of Metropolitan Community Churches, 5300 Santa Monica Blvd. #304, Los Angeles, CA 90029. (213) 464-5100. Listing of gay-oriented churches and groups throughout the United States.

National religious groups with local chapters for lesbians and gays who are Mormon, Lutheran, Seventh Day Adventist, Unitarian, Methodist, Baptist, Presbyterian, Church of Christ and Evangelicals are listed in the Gayellow Pages.

Asian American Lesbian & Gay Men's Network, Box 29627, Philadelphia, PA 19144. (215) 849-4612.

National Coalition of Black Lesbians and Gays, Box 2490, Washington, DC 20013. (202) 265-7117.

Paz y Liberacion, Box 600063, Houston, TX 77260. Information network for Third World Gay Liberation: Latin America, Africa, Middle East, Asia.

Trikon, Box 60536, Palo Alto, CA 94306-0536. (408) 729-4730. South Asia support group: India, Pakistan, Bangladesh, Sri Lanka, Bhutan, Tibet.

Families, Youth, and Seniors

Federation of Parents and Friends of Lesbians and Gays, Inc. (Parents FLAG), P.O. Box 20308, Denver, CO 80220. (303) 321-2270 or (213) 472-8952. Newsletter and referrals to chapters throughout the U.S. offering rap groups, meetings, parent peer counseling, speakers bureaus, library, audio and video cassettes.

Gay & Lesbian Parents Coalition, International, P.O. Box 50360, Washington, DC 20004. (703) 548-3238. Support groups, referrals to local chapters, and a newsletter.

Lesbian Mothers National Defense Fund, P.O. Box 21567, Seattle, WA 98111. (206) 325-2643. Provides legal, financial, and emotional support for custody cases, as well as referral services.

Senior Action in a Gay Environment (SAGE), P.O. Box 115, New York, NY 10023. Network of social services for older lesbians and gay men. Resource list of lesbian and gay aging groups.

Sexual Minority Youth Assistance League (SMYAL), 1638 R St. N.W. #2, Washington, DC 20009. (202) 232-7506. Youth service agency providing referral and counseling services to lesbian, gay, bisexual, transvestite and transsexual youth.

National Gay Youth Network, P.O. Box 846, San Francisco, CA 94114. A clearinghouse for information about lesbian/gay youth groups.

Gay Pen Pals, c/o Alyson Publications, 40 Plympton St., Boston, MA 02118. Gay youth under 21 can write for guidelines to get a pen pal.

Mail Order

Naiad Press, Inc., P.O. Box 10543, Tallahassee, FL 32302. (904) 549-9322. Largest lesbian publishing company in the U.S. Write for mail-order catalogue.

Giovanni's Room, 345 S. 12th St., Philadelphia, PA 19107. (800) 222-6996. Great mail-order book catalogue.

The Whole Gay Catalogue, from: Lambda Rising, 1625 Connecticut Ave. N.W., Washington, DC 20009. (202) 462-6969.

Womankind Books, 5 Kivey St., Huntington Station, New York, NY 11746. (212) 427-1289. Mail order catalogue with over 300 books, records and videos.

A few of the publications of
THE NAIAD PRESS, INC.
P.O. Box 10543 ● Tallahassee, Florida 32302
Phone (904) 539-9322
Mail orders welcome. Please include 15% postage.

LESBIAN CROSSROADS by Ruth Baetz. 276 pp. Contemporary
Lesbian lives.   ISBN 0-941483-21-5 $9.95

BEFORE STONEWALL: THE MAKING OF A GAY AND
LESBIAN COMMUNITY by Andrea Weiss & Greta Schiller.
96 pp., 25 illus.   ISBN 0-941483-20-7   7.95

WE WALK THE BACK OF THE TIGER by Patricia A. Murphy.
192 pp. Romantic Lesbian novel/beginning women's movement.
                                                  ISBN 0-941483-13-4   8.95

SUNDAY'S CHILD by Joyce Bright. 216 pp. Lesbian athletics, at
last the novel about sports.   ISBN 0-941483-12-6   8.95

OSTEN'S BAY by Zenobia N. Vole. 204 pp. Sizzling adventure
romance set on Bonaire.   ISBN 0-941483-15-0   8.95

LESSONS IN MURDER by Claire McNab. 216 pp. 1st in a stylish
mystery series.   ISBN 0-941483-14-2   8.95

YELLOWTHROAT by Penny Hayes. 240 pp. Margarita, bandit,
kidnaps Julia.   ISBN 0-941483-10-X   8.95

SAPPHISTRY: THE BOOK OF LESBIAN SEXUALITY by
Pat Califia. 3d edition, revised. 208 pp.   ISBN 0-941483-24-X   8.95

CHERISHED LOVE by Evelyn Kennedy. 192 pp. Erotic
Lesbian love story.   ISBN 0-941483-08-8   8.95

LAST SEPTEMBER by Helen R. Hull. 208 pp. Six stories & a
glorious novella.   ISBN 0-941483-09-6   8.95

THE SECRET IN THE BIRD by Camarin Grae. 312 pp. Striking,
psychological suspense novel.   ISBN 0-941483-05-3   8.95

TO THE LIGHTNING by Catherine Ennis. 208 pp. Romantic
Lesbian 'Robinson Crusoe' adventure.   ISBN 0-941483-06-1   8.95

THE OTHER SIDE OF VENUS by Shirley Verel. 224 pp.
Luminous, romantic love story.   ISBN 0-941483-07-X   8.95

DREAMS AND SWORDS by Katherine V. Forrest. 192 pp.
Romantic, erotic, imaginative stories.   ISBN 0-941483-03-7   8.95

MEMORY BOARD by Jane Rule. 336 pp. Memorable novel
about an aging Lesbian couple.   ISBN 0-941483-02-9   8.95

THE ALWAYS ANONYMOUS BEAST by Lauren Wright
Douglas. 224 pp. A Caitlin Reese mystery. First in a series.
                                                  ISBN 0-941483-04-5   8.95

SEARCHING FOR SPRING by Patricia A. Murphy. 224 pp.
Novel about the recovery of love.   ISBN 0-941483-00-2   8.95

DUSTY'S QUEEN OF HEARTS DINER by Lee Lynch. 240 pp.
Romantic blue-collar novel.   ISBN 0-941483-01-0   8.95

PARENTS MATTER by Ann Muller. 240 pp. Parents'
relationships with Lesbian daughters and gay sons.
                                   ISBN 0-930044-91-6   9.95

THE PEARLS by Shelley Smith. 176 pp. Passion and fun in
the Caribbean sun.   ISBN 0-930044-93-2   7.95

MAGDALENA by Sarah Aldridge. 352 pp. Epic Lesbian novel
set on three continents.   ISBN 0-930044-99-1   8.95

THE BLACK AND WHITE OF IT by Ann Allen Shockley.
144 pp. Short stories.   ISBN 0-930044-96-7   7.95

SAY JESUS AND COME TO ME by Ann Allen Shockley. 288
pp. Contemporary romance.   ISBN 0-930044-98-3   8.95

LOVING HER by Ann Allen Shockley. 192 pp. Romantic love
story.   ISBN 0-930044-97-5   7.95

MURDER AT THE NIGHTWOOD BAR by Katherine V.
Forrest. 240 pp. A Kate Delafield mystery. Second in a series.
                                   ISBN 0-930044-92-4   8.95

ZOE'S BOOK by Gail Pass. 224 pp. Passionate, obsessive love
story.   ISBN 0-930044-95-9   7.95

WINGED DANCER by Camarin Grae. 228 pp. Erotic Lesbian
adventure story.   ISBN 0-930044-88-6   8.95

PAZ by Camarin Grae. 336 pp. Romantic Lesbian adventurer
with the power to change the world.   ISBN 0-930044-89-4   8.95

SOUL SNATCHER by Camarin Grae. 224 pp. A puzzle, an
adventure, a mystery — Lesbian romance.   ISBN 0-930044-90-8   8.95

THE LOVE OF GOOD WOMEN by Isabel Miller. 224 pp.
Long-awaited new novel by the author of the beloved *Patience
and Sarah.*   ISBN 0-930044-81-9   8.95

THE HOUSE AT PELHAM FALLS by Brenda Weathers. 240
pp. Suspenseful Lesbian ghost story.   ISBN 0-930044-79-7   7.95

HOME IN YOUR HANDS by Lee Lynch. 240 pp. More stories
from the author of *Old Dyke Tales.*   ISBN 0-930044-80-0   7.95

EACH HAND A MAP by Anita Skeen. 112 pp. Real-life poems
that touch us all.   ISBN 0-930044-82-7   6.95

SURPLUS by Sylvia Stevenson. 342 pp. A classic early Lesbian
novel.   ISBN 0-930044-78-9   6.95

PEMBROKE PARK by Michelle Martin. 256 pp. Derring-do
and daring romance in Regency England.   ISBN 0-930044-77-0   7.95

THE LONG TRAIL by Penny Hayes. 248 pp. Vivid adventures
of two women in love in the old west.   ISBN 0-930044-76-2   8.95

THE PRICE OF SALT by Claire Morgan. 288 pp. A milestone
novel, a beloved classic.   ISBN 0-930044-49-5   8.95

AGAINST THE SEASON by Jane Rule. 224 pp. Luminous,
complex novel of interrelationships.   ISBN 0-930044-48-7   8.95

LOVERS IN THE PRESENT AFTERNOON by Kathleen
Fleming. 288 pp. A novel about recovery and growth.
                                              ISBN 0-930044-46-0   8.95

TOOTHPICK HOUSE by Lee Lynch. 264 pp. Love between
two Lesbians of different classes.   ISBN 0-930044-45-2   7.95

MADAME AURORA by Sarah Aldridge. 256 pp. Historical
novel featuring a charismatic "seer."   ISBN 0-930044-44-4   7.95

CURIOUS WINE by Katherine V. Forrest. 176 pp. Passionate
Lesbian love story, a best-seller.   ISBN 0-930044-43-6   8.95

BLACK LESBIAN IN WHITE AMERICA by Anita Cornwell.
141 pp. Stories, essays, autobiography.   ISBN 0-930044-41-X   7.50

CONTRACT WITH THE WORLD by Jane Rule. 340 pp.
Powerful, panoramic novel of gay life.   ISBN 0-930044-28-2   7.95

YANTRAS OF WOMANLOVE by Tee A. Corinne. 64 pp.
Photos by noted Lesbian photographer.   ISBN 0-930044-30-4   6.95

MRS. PORTER'S LETTER by Vicki P. McConnell. 224 pp.
The first Nyla Wade mystery.   ISBN 0-930044-29-0   7.95

TO THE CLEVELAND STATION by Carol Anne Douglas.
192 pp. Interracial Lesbian love story.   ISBN 0-930044-27-4   6.95

THE NESTING PLACE by Sarah Aldridge. 224 pp. A
three-woman triangle—love conquers all!   ISBN 0-930044-26-6   7.95

THIS IS NOT FOR YOU by Jane Rule. 284 pp. A letter to a
beloved is also an intricate novel.   ISBN 0-930044-25-8   8.95

FAULTLINE by Sheila Ortiz Taylor. 140 pp. Warm, funny,
literate story of a startling family.   ISBN 0-930044-24-X   6.95

THE LESBIAN IN LITERATURE by Barbara Grier. 3d ed.
Foreword by Maida Tilchen. 240 pp. Comprehensive bibliography.
Literary ratings; rare photos.   ISBN 0-930044-23-1   7.95

ANNA'S COUNTRY by Elizabeth Lang. 208 pp. A woman
finds her Lesbian identity.   ISBN 0-930044-19-3   6.95

PRISM by Valerie Taylor. 158 pp. A love affair between two
women in their sixties.   ISBN 0-930044-18-5   6.95

These are just a few of the many Naiad Press titles — we are the oldest and
largest lesbian/feminist publishing company in the world. Please request a
complete catalog. We offer personal service; we encourage and welcome
direct mail orders from individuals who have limited access to bookstores
carrying our publications.